# Deborah Sampson
## The Girl Who Went to War

Marilyn Gilbert Komechak

*"Let Your Life Speak."*

An old Quaker saying

*"All adventure, especially into
new territory, are scary."*

Sally Ride, Astronaut

*"Life shrinks or expands in proportion to one's courage."*

Anais Nin, Author

## Dedication

For my "Go-To Girls": Kimberly Komechak, Terry Murphy, Karen Kearney-Komechak, Jayme Begnaud Komechak, Barbara Lee Smith, and for all boys and girls everywhere who have a dream...

# Acknowledgments

My appreciation to two outstanding Deborah scholars and history detectives, Alfred F. Young and Cora Cheney. Your primary research made the difference.

To all the people on the readers' panel who read the manuscript in rough draft form. My heartfelt thanks to each of you. Your suggestions were invaluable.

Olyve Abbott
Linda Austin
Bruce Benbow
Glynis Benbow-Niemier
Virginiae Blackmon
Taylor Burgett
Lois Frazier
Christina Gilbert
Ann Heinz
Cynthia Pyle Howell
Neena Kahlon
Karen Leihy Kaskel
George Komechak
Kimberly Komechak
Russel Komechak
Diane McCartney
Brenda (B.K.) McCollum
Harriette O'Connor
Tom O'Connor
Bunny Pearson
Paul Pearson
Joy Silvers
Troy Silvers
Judie Silvers
Barbara Smith
Jennie Smith
Jo Anna Smith
Julie Smith

Stephanie Smith
Barbara Hoyt Southwell
Dennis Tuck
Jo Denton Tuck
Tracey Wood Mince
Taylor Burgett

Special thanks to Fort Worth Writers. You told me you wanted to live in Deborah's experience, and kept after me until you felt some satisfaction. And, of course, there's no way I'd have completed her story without your interest and kind but persistent prodding!

# Contents

# Deborah Sampson Timeline
(The Five Periods of Her Life)

## Part 1:  1760 - 1781

1760—Deborah's birth, December 17 in Plympton, Massachusetts

1765—Father deserts family. Deborah is sent to live and work for her mother's cousin.

1768—At age eight she is a maid to 80-year-old Widow Thatcher

1770—Deborah, age ten, works as a servant for a Middleborough family.

1778-80—Deborah earns her living as a teacher and as a weaver of fine cloth.

1780-81—Makes an unsuccessful attempt to enlist in the Army as "Timothy Thayer."

1780-82—Third Baptist Church withdraws her name from membership for disguising herself in men's clothing. Succeeds in second attempt as "Robert Shurtliff."

## Part 2: 1782-1784

1782—Joins Light Infantrymen at West Point. Is wounded at Tarrytown and chosen as General Patterson's aide.

1783—Falls ill in Philadelphia. Dr. Barnabas Binney helps her win honorable discharge. Musters out on November 3rd from 4th Massachusetts Regiment at West Point, New York.

## Part 3: 1784-1797

1784—Returns home to try to win back her mother's approval. Hires on as a farm hand. *New York Gazette* tells her story but withholds her name.

1785—Marries Benjamin Gannett on April 7th in Sharon, MA. Bears three children in five years.

1791—Asks Massachusetts Legislature for back pay for time served as a soldier in the American Revolution.

1792—Again petitions Massachusetts soldier's back pay. Adopts Susanna Shepherd.

## Part 4: 1797-1827

1797—Biographer Herman Mann writes Deborah's story. Poet Philip Freneau writes an ode in her honor.

1802-03—Is the first American woman to receive pay for a public lecture tour. Invited to stay in the homes of her former Army officers.

1804—A neighbor, Paul Revere, writes a letter on her behalf requesting a pension.

1805—Deborah is the first woman to wear an Army uniform and to receive a pension, $48.00 a year, for her military service.

1818—A new military "Pension Act" increases her pension to $96.00 a year.

1827—April 29th, Deborah Sampson Gannett dies in Sharon, MA

## Part 5: 1866

1866—Biographer Dr. John Adams Vinton writes Deborah's memoirs and includes some untruths.

## Afterword: 1902-Current

1902—On the 100th anniversary of Deborah's speaking tour, a dinner is held in her honor at Sharon Town Hall.

1944—In Baltimore, MD, a WWII Liberty Ship is launched, named the "Deborah Gannett."

1948—Deborah's re-application for military pension in 1818 is on America's first "Freedom Train."

1976—Deborah Sampson is remembered with honor in the United States Bicentennial celebrations. Texas Boys' Choir sings a song about her.

1982—Massachusetts Governor King names Deborah Sampson as state's heroine.
Sharon Public Library places a statue of Deborah at its entrance.

2004—Deborah's legacy-On May 29, 2004, a memorial is dedicated to all who fought in World War II. Three quotes from women who served were to have been inscribed on the granite panels. Only one quote has been saved, that of Col. Oveta Culp Hobby, "Women who stepped up were measured as citizens of the nation, not as women... this was a people's war and everyone was in it."

Military Army Dress
Courtesy of the Commonwealth Museum Massachusetts
The Source Booklet 1997

# Chapter I

## Private Deborah Sampson

*What have I gotten myself into?* Bobby rammed another bullet down the muzzle of her musket. She bent low to escape the frightening orange flash of musket fire. The hoarse shouts of men mixed with the roar of cannon. Fear trickled down her spine her heart thudding. The battle raged on in smoke and stench, and she was in the thick of it. British bayonets flashed in the twilight. Word came down from General George Washington how well the Brits used those knives. In the next instant, the commanding officer barked out "charge!"

Bobby panted for breath as her regiment ran out of the woods, and made straight for the crimson British line. Bobby continued to fire and quickly reloaded her musket. *When will my luck run out?* She fought back a wave of panic. William, her friend, had died right in front of her eyes in the last battle, shot through the heart with a musket ball. In the same battle, a ball punched through her coat, and another whizzed through her cap. One more hole, she thought, to join the others in her coat, proof of many narrow escapes. Then in a split second she gathered her courage. *I must fight on—no matter what.*

As she rushed at the redcoats, the acrid smell of gun powder filled her nose and throat. She coughed, her eyes burning. Bobby struggled to hold the musket steady, but it shook in her hands. *Control yourself... or die.*

Bobby's name was really Deborah. She was the only girl in the regiment. But nobody suspected her. To them she was 18-year-old, Robert Shurtliff. That's the name she gave when she signed up. Tall as most of the men, Deborah wore her light wheat-colored hair cut short like theirs. Though she thought their hair looked as if it had been trimmed to the edge of a bowl. Since she looked like them, nobody noticed. They called her "Bobby", and some mocked her as a "blooming boy" noting her smooth skin.

Meanwhile, the battle continued. Out of deepening shadows crows frightened from their roosts, cawed into the gloom as the enemy horsemen charged into the clearing. One of the riders barreled down on her swinging his saber intending to decapitate her. She ducked, but not soon enough. The blade tip scratched a cut across her forehead. Bobby hit the ground hard, knocking the breath out of her. The soldier saw the horseman ride on menacing other soldiers. She crawled away, then gathered herself to keep fighting.

The two armies struggled for hours before the British turned and ran. As the last redcoat disappeared over the hill, Bobby stopped and sank to her knees exhausted.

The girl saw a skin of water and felt she'd die from fatigue and thirst. Yet all the soldiers were warned about the cold water disease and told, "You may lose your life if you drink cold water." Then she saw one of the officers grab a jug out of a soldier's hands as he'd raised it to his lips. The officer warned them all: "Even if you're dying of thirst—drinking water must be boiled over a campfire."

A groan went up from the troops. The officer went on, "Cold river water tainted with decaying fish will poison you—as surely as a bullet that finds its mark kills."

*A lot to remember... it's all too much,* Deborah despaired. Her mouth and throat felt dry as straw. And to make matters worse she might not be able to start a fire as the evening dew dampened everything.

As the secret soldier lay on the ground, she heard the night birds return to the trees. She pressed her back and shoulders into the soft earth. Worn out from the strain and fright of battle, she fell into a ragged sleep,

In the middle of the night Deborah awakened in pain. She remembered her wound, and the horseman's swinging saber. The soldier gingerly touched her fingers to her forehead. She felt something warm and sticky. Although some blood had dried, the saber cut still seeped. Deborah raised her head and looked about for a cloth. In her haversack, a canvas bag, she found a bit of cloth from a first aid kit. The cloth was none too clean. She'd recently cleaned her rifle with it. Hoping she wouldn't get blood poisoning, she pressed the cloth to her forehead. Then she closed her eyes, but sleep did not come. Finally, Deborah stopped trying and stared up at the starless sky with its tilted moon. *There's that lop-sided moon again... the same as I saw the night I left home.*

Thoughts of having left her home and the Thomases made her sad. Yes, she served them, been indentured to them, since she was ten. They didn't always understand her, but they'd been kind. And the Thomas boys Ransom and Jeremiah—how she missed their pestering.

Deborah knew she must sleep. She'd need every ounce of energy for their march tomorrow. When the sun came up, the soldier would have to straighten her shoulders, act the part of a good military man. Now, though, as she re-played the battle in her mind, she felt her heart spasm like a fist slowly opening and closing.

As the clandestine soldier lay on the ground, wounded, she did not let herself sob. She trembled as both fear and pride flooded over her. Deborah put her finger through a hole in her coat—as if to prove to herself it was really there. Then she picked up her hat and looked at the bullet hole. She touched again the still seeping gash on her head. Her fingers showed blood in the moonlight. *War is horrible business. I might get killed.* But tomorrow she must be ready for whatever came her way. Sometime during the night Deborah curled into her blanket and slept.

When the sun crept over the horizon, someone called, "Hey, Bobby, you OK?"

Still groggy with sleep Deborah puzzled, *Who Me?...* Then, coming to herself, *Oh, that's me.* She waved her hand as she struggled to get up.

"Yes, Sir," she yelled back, nodding. The officer turned away to check on the other men. Bobby shook her head to wake herself up but wished she hadn't. Her head ached. Then the soldier muttered to herself, "I've got to tell my feet... get ready to march!"

As the soldier tramped along her head throbbed, and her feet felt like lead. The cold wind reminded her to put on her cap. But the cap didn't fit. It aggravated the wound. Richard, the man next to Deborah said, "You got a swelling the size of a goose egg." It'd be impossible to wear her hat. With one move she cocked it on the back of her head. No officer would give her grief, not after what they'd been through, not over a hat. She hoped....

## Crossing a River of Ice

Deborah's company stayed on the move. As fall turned to winter, they marched south close to enemy territory. At last they came to the Croton River which had become a solid sheet of ice. Deborah, shaking with the chill, felt her blood turn cold as she looked at the ice-locked river.

"Forward men!" their leader yelled motioning them onto the frozen stream. Deborah walked unable to feel her feet. She thought about the danger of frostbite, but she stumbled on. Others were having difficulty, too. The ice covered with slushy snow, made it hard to stay upright. The penetrating wind cut and pushed at the men. Richard fell to his knees. She grabbed his arm and helped him up. Panting hard, their breath formed miniature snowballs in the air. Finally, they reached the opposite shore. Deborah hobbled to a tree stump and sat down to remove her boots.

Deborah said over her shoulder to any who'd listen, "If we rub our feet a bit and get the circulation going..." but a shot rang out as she bent to remove the first boot. They'd been spotted. The enemy fired on them, although they were still in the free zone, or "no man's land." This territory, an area about thirty miles wide, was not held by either of the opposing armies.

The Americans fled in a mad dash back across the dangerous, ice-bound Croton. "Brits play by their own rules," she huffed to the man next to her. She couldn't help but flinch as a bullet whizzed by her neck and struck with a thud into the ice. Smoke lazily curled up from the spot.

Scrambling, the soldiers crawled up the north bank of the river. Looking behind her, she saw the British had given up the chase. "They must have been as cold as we were," she thought. As one, they breathed a grateful sigh of relief. Safety! But there was a somber feel in the air. The men did not joke or laugh. She realized by crossing the river, they'd tempted death. Theirs had been a narrow escape.

Deborah brushed the snow off a large rock and sat down. She'd grown horribly thirsty, again. The thirst she'd had last night came to mind. Fear had a way of parching her mouth. And now, to add insult to injury, her stomach rumbled with hunger. The men looked hungry too, their faces drawn and eyes sunken in their heads. Could things get any worse? Her chin dropped on her chest. *I'll just close my eyes for a minute.* However, she was awakened when she heard heavy footsteps behind her. A soldier rudely clapped her on the shoulder.

"Wake up, Bobby, the Captain's coming."

The officer, mounted on horseback, reined up. He eyed the men. He announced what she feared. "We're low on grub. Vegetables, dairy and livestock are in the South, guarded by the Brits, the very place we were chased out of. The redcoats hope we'll try to come and take it.... They'd like nothing better than to trap us in the south, though what they claim isn't theirs."

The men grumbled and stared off in a southerly direction. "I need three soldiers, men good on horseback to sneak in and raid their camp." A deep silence followed.

Deborah watched her hand go up as if it belonged to someone else. "I'll go, Sir," she volunteered, using her deepest voice.

"We might as well go too," a couple of others spoke up. "We'll be back tonight with some vittles worth eating." Soon the three of them, their heads together, worked on a plan. They agreed a stealth raid would be risky. They'd have to keep their wits about them. They talked about how the low-intensity warfare was about to heat up. But hungry Deborah could almost taste the ham.

## The Danger of Discovery

But all the while, the secret soldier knew she had to be careful. Women were not welcome in the army. The law in the 1700's made it illegal. Women were supposed to stay home, not shoot redcoats with a musket on a hill far away.

Her heart raced when she thought about another girl who enlisted as a boy. That girl had upset the officers at table when serving coffee. She'd forgotten and curtsied—not something any man would do. The men jumped up knocking over their chairs. They chased her from the room. The camp was in an uproar for days. People gossiped about other girls, too. One girl, Deborah heard, who became an officer, went to jail for two months. Then there were the girls who joined the army with the very boys they were forbidden to marry. They, too, were shamed, drummed out, and sent home—or placed in jail.

Deborah did not want her family to turn against her. As for the Thomases they'd taken her in as their servant when she was ten. Her father had disappeared, and was never heard from again. Her mother could not provide for the children by herself. Deborah felt lucky the army provided her with food and shelter, even if soldiering meant hard work and exposure to danger. She knew she worked every bit as hard as the Thomases boys. *Still, more than anything I want to make my mother proud. And the Thomases too. But I have to risk it. To do something—to make my own way—after all, my ancestors had courage.*

She'd heard the story from her mother how their relatives came over on the Mayflower to settle the new world. One man was governor of Plymouth Colony. Everyone knew William Bradford, Miles Standish and John Alden.

*No, I must not be found out.* The thought of their combined anger heaped on her head made her quake. Yet, some part of her refused to be numbed by fear. She'd always known that within her was a solid supply of spunk and daring.

That night shivering in the cold her eyes misted over. She wished she could play once more with the Thomases children, Ransom and Jeremiah. They were like pesky brothers. She rubbed her cold hands together as if she were at their fireside popping corn and playing games.

Her mind drifted back to her room in the Thomases' loft. So much had changed since those nights when she'd taught herself to read and write.

# Chapter II

## Life as an Indentured Servant

"Please, Sir, let me go to school when the boys go. I'll do extra work. I'll do anything," Deborah pestered Deacon Thomas. But his silence was his answer. She was their servant, and so he refused. She ached to learn. The Thomas boys went off to school without her. She felt that ache all the way to her toes.

Each morning as she sat milking, the boys ran down the lane to the schoolhouse. She did not see them again until noon. After lunch they helped with more chores. Then away they went back to school. In the afternoon Deborah listened for their voices in the lane. Hardly able to wait to find out what they learned that day, the eager girl caught them as they tumbled in the door.

"Here's a glass of buttermilk for each of you. And some warm-from-the-oven molasses cookies!" Deborah stressed the last words drawing them out. "But before you take a sip or a bite, tell me what you learned." The boys knew she had the best of them, and began to recite their lessons.

But Deacon Thomas still admonished her, "You can't be spared from the house and barn." There was, however, another reason. "You must be careful, child. I know you like to read. But reading causes brain fever in girls." He fixed her with a stern eye.

True, most people in Middleborough thought schooling for girls unimportant, even dangerous. "I don't think they're right," she grumbled as she pitched hay and churned the butter. "I've read for hours in the loft and never felt the least bit feverish."

Deborah enjoyed writing down her thoughts. It helped her form her own opinions, and to compare them with those of others. In this way, she began to have confidence in her feelings and ideas. "Well, I know what I believe," she said to the chickens as she scattered corn. The hens cackled and clucked their merry agreement.

Her longing to go to school grew even stronger. But the boys grew impatient of her questions.

"We're tired of talking about school," they said. "Go hunting with us, Deb. Sneak some ham from the smokehouse to take with us. That way we can stay out longer."

"OK, but then you've got to tell me everything you learned at school this week."

"Sure, Deb. You've got our word on it," they promised as they ran out the door.

This is the time Deborah became expert in robbing smokehouses—a skill that came in handy later. And though try as he might, Deacon Thomas never caught the thief.

She taught herself all the things the boys knew, and a whole lot more. She even began teaching a few younger children who lived near-by.

People in Middleborough heard about this and said, "Deborah you are quite a scholar—for a girl." Still, they shook their heads and raised their eyebrows. "That's a girl who knows too much for her own good," they judged. "Females don't reason well." But something inside her knew differently.

In those days, most agreed only men could understand religion, government, science, and the natural world. Still, Deborah never stopped searching for answers to her own questions.

She wished she could travel. The servant girl wanted to see Boston, Philadelphia, and New York. Deborah confided to her church deacon Mr. Conant. He said those three cities are magical. And, he's been to Providence and to Newport, Rhode Island on the sea. She loved to hear him tell what he's seen on his travels. *But that's not enough for me. I want to see for myself."*

She wrote down all the things she wanted to see and do. To keep her dreams alive, she borrowed books from anyone who came by.

One day Mr. Conant, dropped in for a cup of tea. He knew how much the girl wanted to see the great cities of America.

"Deborah, I have a gift for you. It's a book I've read many times—a book I've had since I was a boy. It's called *Gulliver's Travels*. With this you can scratch your travel itch," he smiled.

12

"Someday you can write a book of your own. Call it 'Deborah's Travels.' Who knows what wonders the future holds for you."

Deborah leaped to her feet nearly knocking over the tea table. "Whoa, girl. Easy. I must say, it's good to see you smile again." Deborah read and re-read the book until its cover almost fell off.

But Mrs. Thomas complained, "You're always hammering on some book. And why waste time scratching on paper?" Deborah only smiled demurely and ran off to pick black raspberries for a pie.

Many a night her candle in the loft burned late. "Someday, I'll become a teacher", she muttered. "No one cares if a spinster knows how to read and write. And I don't care a fig about marriage. *Pshaw!* After all, as for having kids, I've practically raised those Thomas boys."

As Deborah wrote down her thoughts she became more intense, and pressed so hard on the pen the quill-end broke off. Ink splattered all over her secrets. "All the better," she whispered to the ceiling. "The boys won't be able to read it if it falls into their hands. They are pretty nosey—not that they want to spend any time reading," her merry laugh sounded in the rafters. And every evening she faithfully wrote in her diary, the movement from her quill pen flickering in the candle light. On many evenings Deborah wrote with only the wind to murmur encouragement.

But one night, as soon as she wrote, "Dear Diary," a flood of words spilled onto the paper. *What will become of me? I've got to sort myself out*, and so she dipped the quill once more in the ink. "Teaching would be fine, if I'm ever offered that job," she wrote, "but what then?"

As she wrote, certain questions haunted her. How could she make her dreams to learn, to understand the world and to travel come true?" Deborah searched her mind and heart for answers.

Then she gathered her wits, and made a list. She wrote down her good acts on one side of the paper. On the other side, she wrote her bad thoughts and bad deeds. Writing things down helped her think as it always had. Though, she confessed, stealing ham from the smokehouse—that made her feel guilty. Stealing hams fell on the bad side.

Often she stopped to sharpen the quill with her knife. She didn't want the mess if the point broke again. Now, though, the quill was too short to continue. "Hummm... well, tomorrow I'll make another one, and a spare," she murmured sleepily.

It had grown late. One candle and the stub of another guttered before going out.

In time the girl's diary led her to some surprising conclusions. They were especially surprising for the time in which she lived. Deborah would eventually act on her beliefs—as those who knew her would soon find out.

## Deborah's Ideas

The Thomases, and people in the Puritan Congregational Church, worried about Deborah. "Why were there so many different religions when they all worship the same God?" she asked. They scratched their heads and turned away. "What a silly girl—asking such a question," they grumbled to each other.

But Deborah kept her own ideas about religion. Her church and the town's people tried to "set her right." Deborah listened with respect, but made up her own mind.

"Our town should not be taxed to support only one church. Support them all or support none of them." But what she said next got her into hot water:

"Each man and woman should be able to decide where, if and when they will worship."

Deacon Thomas said, "You're a willful girl. Why are you so stubborn?" he wanted to know.

Still, the Thomases continued to give her the same help and care they gave their own children—except for education. Mrs. Thomas told her, "We count on you. You're a hard worker, and a dependable girl—in spite of your hardheaded ways."

"You're like our big sister," the boys chorused, jumping up and down, and yanked her braids. She knew then what she'd always known—they considered her part of the family.

"You're all little scallywags," she said, chasing the boys out into the yard and around the pear tree.

When she was sixteen, Deacon Thomas had given her a small bit of land to graze one sheep. "Now you can use your spinning and weaving skills. The ladies in the village say you weave the finest cloth for one so young. Keep the bit of the money you earn," he'd told her. "Put it toward a marriage dowry, for you have none. And money from the sale of extra eggs you may also keep." The girl felt like hugging him, but didn't dare. Joyfully, she skipped about the kitchen.

She always remembered Deacon Thomas's gift. In time she saved and bought another sheep, and started a little flock of her own.

After shearing her sheep, Deborah spun and then wove the wool into cloth. She kept the egg money in an old tin cup beneath her mattress. From time to time she added to it with earnings from her weaving. The girl's weaving skills would, in time, change Deborah's life.

A strong and healthy teenager, she knew how to take care of a house and farm. And she knew how to take care of children. "She'll make the perfect wife," the Thomases agreed.

By being diligent, Deborah taught herself all of the subjects Ransom and Jeremiah learned in school. She taught herself so well, the people in town asked her to teach in the school. They excused hiring a girl on the basis that all the men teachers had gone off to fight the British.

The timing was good. Her indenture, her service to the Thomases, neared its end. When she heard about the offer to teach, Deborah wrote in her diary, "Well, there is more than one way to get into school. She threw her head back and laughed at the irony of it all. Hearing her merry laugh up in the loft, the Thomases couldn't help but smile.

## Anyone for Tea?

In 1774, the British planned to put a tax on tea. The King of England said they had no choice. They *must* pay.

"It already costs too much," the colonists complained. "Tea is a special treat. We don't have nearly as much as we want, now!" Like the Thomases, most homes kept their tea in a chest under lock and key. Only the lady of the house had the key. Tea was a precious item.

Around tables and firesides, people fumed. "Something's got to be done. This tax is unfair. That knuckleheaded King is taking our rights away," Deacon Thomas snorted.

King George felt the colonies were not profitable enough. He decided to charge them more for all English goods, including tea. Suddenly things took a turn for the worse. The colonists threw a large shipment of precious English tea overboard into the Boston Harbor. They were angry because the King had imposed a harsh tax.

That evening at supper, Deborah laughed when she heard the news. "Wish I'd have been there to see that. It's a jolly good trick." She liked how Americans took such daring action.

She imagined herself one of the men disguised as an Indian. Deborah wore buckskin and painted her face. She took one of the feathers being passed around and stuck it in her hair. She stole with the others onto an English ship at night. The only sound, water slapping against the wooden hull. The moon, like the orb of an eye, looked on.

They each grabbed up sacks of English tea and tossed them overboard. Water sprayed up in a perfect fountain as each bag smacked the water. Then they rowed in their canoes to the next ship. Deborah helped them dump tea from not one, but all three British ships.

"Deborah, what are you thinking?" the deacon asked, as he spooned more roasted potatoes onto his plate.

"Well, Sir, more than tea's been stirred-up in Boston. Maybe, now, the British will have to go fishing for their tea." Deborah laughed at her own joke.

"Oh, Deborah, only you would think of that," Mrs. Thomas sighed, worry crossing her face. "What if the prank back-fires?"

Deacon Thomas looked up from his paper, nodding. "Not everyone thinks the prank funny. Now we're really in hot water. No ships can dock at Boston Harbor. I read that people are starving. There's no food or tea coming to them. Ol' King George says he'll punish them for ruining all that tea. He's already put some men in jail. Besides, he says the people of Boston must pay—not only for the ruined tea—but for the tax on it besides!"

The three of them stared at each other. Deborah found her voice. "I don't think England should be bullying us. After all, she calls herself our mother country! I'm not against rules, and even some taxes" she went on, "when they're for everyone's benefit."

The deacon caught his wife's eye. Deborah was no end of surprises. The girl astonished them with her knowledge and keen insight. Even though she'd not been to school, she'd taught herself to read and kept up with all the news.

Deborah drummed her fingers on the table. Straightening she looked up at Deacon Thomas. "Please, Sir, could we could take some corn to the people in Boston? They can grind it into corn meal. We've got extra in the crib from this season."

Deacon Thomas eyes widened. Slowly he laid aside his paper. The girl held her breath. Had she gone too far? She let go of her breath only after she saw him smile.

"If you'll help me sack and load the corn into the wagon, you can go with me."

Deborah almost tipped over as she rocked back in her chair at the good news. She couldn't believe her good luck. Her first patriotic act and Boston in the bargain!

## Deborah, Young Patriot

After supper and the dishes done, Deacon Thomas and Deborah went out to pack the wagon. The girl patted the big bay and stroked his black mane. Bob pranced a bit as if sensing her excitement. "Ol' boy, we're depending on you!" Bob arched his neck and whickered. The girl picked up her brown felt hat and jammed on her head. She eagerly leapt up to take her place on the wagon seat. The deacon climbed up onto the seat and took the reins. They'd loaded all the corn they could spare.

The wagon bumped along the rough road. But the deacon kept Bob at a steady pace. Deborah's teeth jarred when the wagon hit hidden roots and holes in the road. She dodged overhanging branches, putting up her hands to shield her face. Once her hat almost blew off before she could grab it. But nothing could dim her excitement. She was going to Boston.

Red and gold maple leaves showered around them in the fall air. And though the breeze felt cool, Deacon Thomas frequently rubbed his sleeve across his forehead. Deborah also felt sweat on her brow.

No doubt about it. They were on a mission to bring food to the starving people of Boston. And she hoped against hope, they'd not get caught.

"Hang on, girl. *Blast* these country roads." With that, the wagon gave another bone-jarring lurch. The deacon, his face filled with concern yelled, *haw*. He yanked the reins left to avoid another sizable hole. The holes had deepened, washed out by hard rains. The girl was relieved as the closer they came to the city, the road grew wider and smoother.

Deacon Thomas pulled back on the reins as they approached Campbell's Inn. "We've got to water Bob and give him some rest. Then we'll be on our way again."

Deborah stepped down and walked around a bit to stretch her legs. The Deacon was in deep conversation with a man she thought to be Mr. Campbell. Then after a wave goodbye the Deacon joined Deborah on the wagon seat. Bob set off at a brisk trot.

After hours of traveling, they stopped and climbed down from the wagon. Deborah stretched her back and legs and looked around. They were on the outskirts of the city. Deborah stood on tip-toe trying to peer through the trees. There it was, there was Boston! The Deacon handed her his spy glass. "Look carefully, Girl, and you'll see redcoats at the town entrance."

She saw the redcoats. She could see the dust in the air from the city streets as wagons and carriages rolled along. But what was this other feeling? Something felt, well, not only different, but strange—like thrill mixed up with fear. Her breath quickened and goose bumps rose on her arms.

"Sorry, Deborah, but we'd best not go much farther." *We've come all this way and now I can't go into Boston?* Her heart sank and she felt a frown crease her brow. "I know you're disappointed, but remember when we stopped at Campbell's Inn to water Bob and give him a rest? The man at the Inn has family in Boston. They had word there'd be a man to meet anyone bringing food. He'd be wearing a sprig of evergreen on his hat. He said he'd send a runner to the man, and that he would be waiting for us."

Some distance away was a two-story white rooming house. A large chestnut tree grew near the house. Deacon Thomas pointed, "See that man napping under the tree with his hat down over his eyes? He'll not jump up to greet us because he doesn't want the

British to know what he's up to. And see, there's that sprig of green.... The redcoats have guards around the city to prevent any more problems with unruly citizens. But they don't suspect him. They've been told he's a king's man, loyal to King George."

"Well, he looks perfectly innocent to me—just a man who needs a nap."

"That's what the redcoats think too. They think he's a Tory—one who sides with the British. Little do they know he is a Whig—an American patriot. His trick works well... so far. He's a friend of the Campbells who own the inn. He'll take our corn to the folks who need it most."

The man lifted his hat momentarily. "That's our signal," the deacon said. The girl and the deacon quietly slipped around to the back of the house. They left the corn in a little shed, and covered the bags with an old blanket.

Running back, the girl jumped onto the wagon. The strange sense came again and made her shiver—something she could not see, feel but not touch. Her heart thudded. Panic rose in her as she looked around at the house and the woods. What if those awful redcoats are spying on them right now? Out of the corner of her eye, she saw something move in the trees. Then, for a moment, she thought she heard musket fire—faint popping sounds in the distance. What was the Deacon waiting for? Forget Boston, she wanted to go home *now*.

She watched as the man under the tree scratched a map in the dirt with a stick. Deacon Thomas nodded, thanked him, and hurried to the wagon. There was trouble in his eyes, but he smiled.

"We'd best leave now. He says more citizens have been put in prison. The city, and countryside are thick with redcoats."

Deacon Thomas slapped the horse's rump with the reins. "The man told me how we could avoid that two-rut road that brought us here." Turning the wagon into a byway, he coaxed the tired horse, "*Get-up, Bob. Get-up boy*. You'll get no water and a rest until we reach the inn again."

They'd hardly started when the deacon had to rein in the horse. A man with a shepherd's crook coaxed a bleating flock of sheep across the road in front of them. He waved a friendly hand toward them. The sun was quickly setting. The sweat from her hatband stung her eyes. Oh! please, please hurry, she thought. It took several minutes for the wooly animals to cross. Finally, they started again.

The new road was crooked and the going slow, but eventually they turned onto a better one. They swept along the shadow darkened lane, the horse in a lather. Deborah looked into the gloom along the road, her mind racing. *What was that moving in the trees? What if they catch us? We could be put into prison or worse... shot. Will we ever make it home?*

But in the sky the moon moved with them, to momentarily disappear behind a few straggly clouds. Deborah felt like blowing a kiss to the crystal orb, glad for the light. Still, she had no idea where she was or how much further they had to go.

They'd only just turned into the barn lot when Mrs. Thomas, lantern in hand, rushed up. "Thank goodness you're back and safe." She sat the lantern down and gathered them both in her arms. "There's shocking news! A man on horseback raced through the countryside telling of a massacre in Boston. British soldiers shot some men."

Deborah caught her breath. They both stared at Mrs. Thomas, stunned. She went on, "A crowd cursed the British guards... tried to free the men in prison... the very ones who dumped the tea in the harbor. Now the redcoats shot some men dead." Deborah knew, then, the popping sounds she'd heard were the muskets from the massacre. It was the start of war, the Thomases agreed.

Deborah wanted to stay up and hear the whole story, but the Deacon told her she should go to bed. Reluctantly, Deborah climbed the ladder to the loft. She tossed and turned on her straw mattress, her mind raced sleep evading her. For now she felt that taking corn to the starving people of Boston was only a start. Something had to be done, and soon.

Alone the next day, Deborah worked in the pasture with Bob until she stopped to rest. But she'd only sat for a few minutes before her thoughts had her jumping up. With a stick across her shoulder, she marched around the pasture. She spoke her wish to fight for freedom to no one, except Bob.

She thought how she and Bob could ride into battle together. "After all, the 'Maid of Orleans'—Joan of Arc—was a poor girl, too." Bob whinnied his approval, pawed the ground ready to go.

"She even went to the French King. 'I beg you; give me your army to battle the British at Orleans.'"

In Deborah's imagination, she *was* the Maid... though she carried the Colonial Flag. Then the horse stepped on a stick of wood. Its crack brought Deborah came back to reality with a gasp—just before the Maid was to be burned at the stake.

Danger lay ahead. Deborah could tell by the way the men talked, and from the look in their eyes, and by hearing about the massacre in Boston. She felt, for the first time, fear for her own safety. She remembered the night they returned from Boston. A clammy fear moistened her palms as she recalled the popping sound of the guns. Now men lay dead.

# Chapter III

## The Dream

Deborah tried to calm herself as she reached for her quill pen. She knew the dream was important and wanted to write it down. She'd awakened in a sweat, panting from a terrifying nightmare. The same dream came to her twice before. And she knew that Americans believed if a dream came three times, it would come true.

Deborah's dream first came two days before the Battle of Lexington on April 15, 1775. It was a battle that changed lives forever, and marked the beginning of the American Revolution.

She had no trouble recalling the vivid reoccurring dream as she wrote:

"I am walking along a road, and see the sky is a cloudless blue. I feel the warm sun on my face. Everything is as usual. Farmers work in their fields as the cows graze. A soft breeze blows moving the leaves on the trees. Suddenly, the sky turns black. Thunder blasts. I stop and stand without moving. Then, there's a deafening crash. Startled, I look up. Lightning divides the dark sky, spreading like a horse's tail in the wind. I put my hand over my nose. There's a stink in the air like burning sulphur."

"Water rises up, tall as a mountain. Ships smash against one another sinking beneath the waves. Then a monstrous serpent—a snake—rolls out of the ocean. It comes at me! I race for home through streets running with blood."

"I reach home and dive under my bed covers. But the great snake finds me. His mouth is wide and flashing razor-sharp teeth. His eyes are balls of fire. I am so scared I almost faint. Help! Help! I call, but I can't make a sound."

"Then I hear a voice. It is Deborah from the Bible. 'Arise, stand on your feet. Gird yourself. Prepare yourself to meet your enemy.'

At that, the snake shrinks and tries to leave. I hit him until he breaks into pieces. I wake up crying, shaking and gasping for breath."

The voice of the Biblical Deborah stayed in her mind, as did the vivid dream. Years passed before she told the dream to anyone. But Deborah felt sure the nightmares were about the war.

## Talk of War

One day in late October, Deborah walked the two miles to Middleborough to deliver eggs and pick up mail at Sproat's Inn. Her coat was warm, and she enjoyed the fresh crisp air.

The Deacon had given her a bit more freedom for the constant round of chores. Perhaps it was, she thought, because the end of her indenture drew near. She wondered what it would be like to be free. As she neared Sproat's, her eyes grew wide as she looked around. There was a new sign hanging from the porch rail, "Sons of Liberty Entertained Here."

Deborah knew that Sproat's Inn was one of the places that recruited men for the army. Then, with no one near, Deborah stepped over to the stick used for measuring the height of army recruits. She ran a finger up the length and wondered if she was tall enough to fight. But a man walking up to the inn caused her to step away before she could be seen measuring herself.

"Good day, Mr. Sproat," she called at the door of the inn. "Who are these men?" she asked, pointing to the sign.

"The Sons of Liberty... it's their code name... they're asking everyone not to buy British goods—not until the King changes his mind. He's forcing us to pay more for food, tea and clothes. The British are treating us like we're their servants. By the way, I may have an opportunity for you... come talk to me before you start back home." Mr. Sproat turned and walked back into the inn to help some waiting guests.

After she'd sold the eggs to Mrs. Sproat, the girl went to watch the militia drill on the green—a grassy square in the center of town. A swarm of girls came to watch too. They said the men would soon march to Boston to fight the redcoats.

Deborah saw that each militia man wore an evergreen sprig in his hat. "Washington ordered his men to wear a green bough. It is a

24

badge of rebellion," one girl informed them, tossing her hair. Deborah wanted to stay on and watch, but rather than dawdle, she went to pick up the mail. Then she walked back to the inn. *What did Mr. Sproat mean about giving me an opportunity?*

"Girl," he said, "can you do us a bit of weaving next month? I'll set-up a loom here in this lobby—right where you're standing. I know you have a loom at home but Mrs. Thomas will want to use that one. My wife tells me you're an excellent weaver. I think our militia is going to need more clothes."

Deborah was thrilled by the compliment, and the chance to serve. "I'll have to ask Deacon Thomas, but I'm hopeful think he'll agree."

On the walk home, Deborah found a sprig of evergreen and put it in her hair. She picked up a stick from the roadside. Marching along she imitated the drills she'd seen on the green. Birds in the thickets sang to cheer her on. As she neared home, she tucked the evergreen into the pocket of her skirt. The stick she dropped into the ditch. The Thomases would be most unhappy to see her parading around like a soldier. Besides, she had no real gun. What would she do if a redcoat stopped her on the way home? That thought made her walk faster.

That night, by the fireside and in between the English songs, there was talk of war.

There was a knock on the door. Deacon Thomas opened the door a wee bit to see who was there. "We are the Sons of Liberty."

Deborah had heard of the men. Timothy came from the Thayer family. The other man was Robert Shurtliff. Both men came from Plympton where she was born.

Together the men talked about the rough handling of the colonial citizens by the redcoats. The British army threatened the colonists like a giant bully. There was talk of war by many firesides that night.

Deborah served the men the coffee grounds she'd boiled with water over the fire. She knew they liked tea better, but would enjoy a patriotic cup of coffee.

## Deborah the Weaver

The well-to-do women invited the girl to work at their looms. Deborah lived a short time in each home until the weaving was done. Her reputation grew. Soon she traveled from house to house—an itinerate weaver. Deborah loved the freedom this gave her. Moving around, she had a chance to know each family and to see how they lived.

Why a good weaver can make as much as a man mowing and reaping. Deborah also was fortunate enough to stay in the best homes.

She grew to love fine clothing and china. Though, in time, so much weaving was boring. Deborah became restless as she wondered about her future.

*America's freedom and my freedom are bound together. We're going down the same path. And neither of us knows the outcome.*

## Yankee Doodle

Deborah sat at the edge of the fire on the three-legged milking stool she'd carved herself. The young Thomas boys, Ransom and Jeremiah, drew near to hear her news from Middleborough.

"It's true... Mr. Sproat told me this himself. The British accused some colonists of hiding long guns and powder. They were going to search until they found them. But he said Paul Revere and William Dawes rode out warning everyone. They yelled, 'The British are coming,' at every house and hedgerow! But those fifty Minutemen stopped the enemy at Concord Bridge."

The boys chorused, "*Ohhh*! Tell us more," they begged.

"Well, and here's the truth...." Suddenly Deborah stopped and sniffed the air. "What's that smell?" Then she saw where the odor was coming from and yelled, "Move Ransom, or you're going to scorch your britches!" The littlest boy swatted at his pants, moving out of harm's way. Deborah breathed a sigh of relief. It was close, but he hadn't actually caught fire. He gave Deborah an embarrassed grin as he drew his own small stool up next to hers.

"Go on Deborah," he begged. "I'll be careful."

She shook her head in Ransom's direction before she continued. "The Brits, I heard, loved to sing, '*Yankee Doodle.*' They'll sing it loud and rough with fife and drum. But the problem is, they sang it with a sneer."

"Why do they do that, Deborah?" the littlest boy wanted to know as he leaned on her shoulder.

"Because they think we're country bumpkins. Our men don't have fancy uniforms. But we're smarter than we appear." Deborah shifted her position on the stool and looked off into the distance. How she'd love to show those redcoats what the colonists were made of.

"Go on, Deborah," the oldest youth, Jeremiah, insisted.

"Well, there is more about the song. When the younger men went to Concord to stop the British, two old men stayed behind. They spent the day helping Mrs. Pratt pull weeds and prune the hedge around her cottage.... But then, who should march over the hill and into sight? Six young redcoats! They marched right smart beside a supply wagon.... and they were singing. Well, bellowing is more like it. Can you guess what song they sang?"

"Yes." shouted the boys, "Yankee Doodle!"

Deborah reached over and ruffled their hair. "You are such smart boys!"

"But I spoke first, Deborah," the littlest one said.

"No he didn't," the older insisted.

"Do you two boys what to hear the rest of the story?"

"Please, please, Deb. We'll be quiet," they promised. Ransom stuck his tongue out at Jeremiah who reached to pinch him, but he stopped when Deborah caught his eye.

"Well, the old men eased over to hide behind a hay stack with their muskets. Mrs. Pratt kept right on hoeing weeds, not looking the least perturbed. The enemy passed in front of the house, singing at the top of their lungs—real smart-alecky. One of the old men called out in a wavering voice, 'Throw down your guns or... or we'll shoot.' The redcoats laughed like it was a big joke."

"'What's that you say old fella?' And they kept right on marching and singing at the top of their lungs."

"Then *ca-boom*! The men fired, and killed two of them. The other four soldiers—I can hardly believe this myself—ran right up to Mrs. Pratt. They surrendered to her! Well, Mrs. Pratt did what any sensible woman would do. She handed her hoe to a redcoat to hold, and went inside. There she woke her napping son, a member of the militia. 'Son, put on your officer's coat. I have a present for you.'" The two stepped back outside. The redcoat with the hoe, and his fellow soldiers, looked wild-eyed at the two old men with guns pointed at them.

"Mrs. Pratt said, 'Here's some red-coated devils for you, son. They surrendered to me, but as far as I'm concerned, you can have the lot of them!'"

The boys jumped up and down cheering. They marched around Deborah on her milking stool and sang loudly with pride, "*Yankee Doodle* went to town...*"

Months later, a neighbor boy came to see Deborah. She was busy in the kitchen baking bread when he knocked. He wore a military uniform. "I'm a soldier, now, little girl," he teased.

"You look... good, I guess, though I'm as tall as you. Be quiet now, and show me those drills with the musket." Deborah watched closely as he demonstrated the drills. She asked many questions as they talked with their heads together. Then she slathered some warm bread with butter and put it on a plate for him.

The boy said, "If I didn't know better, I'd think you were going to war yourself. Only, they wouldn't put up with you for a day."

"And why not?"

"First off, you're a girl, and second they couldn't stand your why, why, why—that's why!" Deborah picked up a wooden spoon and chased him out the kitchen door.

That night as she climbed the ladder to her bed in the loft, dread overcame her. Someday Ransom and Jeremiah would clean their guns and mold lead shot. They'd done that before, but for hunting game for the table. She couldn't bear the thought of seeing them march off to war. She was like a big sister to them, and in some ways she felt motherly toward them. Deborah sighed. *I've practically raised those two boys.*

## Daughters of Liberty

In the spring, Deborah began weaving at Sproat's Inn for the soldiers. She felt like she was at the cross roads of the world. Here she heard all the news and gossip of the war. The new recruits talked freely as they played skittles, a game where a wooden ball is thrown to knock down pins.

As Deborah worked at her loom she watched the eight military companies drill. Each man carried a musket, homemade bullets and a powder horn. A man must be at least five feet five inches tall to fire a musket. This was because the musket's ram rod measured five feet long. Deborah noticed each volunteer's height was checked at the measuring post outside Sproat's Inn. The post decided who became a soldier and who did not.

That Saturday morning, Deborah's thoughts flew as fast as her shuttle, a device that carried the thread back and forth between the threads. Looking about, she saw no one. I'll try once again to measure myself, she thought.

Leaving her loom, she slipped away and stood up against the marker. She measured five feet and seven inches. "I'm taller by two inches than most of the fighting men of Massachusetts, New York and New Jersey!" she whispered in glee.

"Well, Deborah, are you getting ready to join the army?" joked Mr. Sproat who had appeared in the doorway. She smiled up at him.

"No, Sir," she responded. "But those redcoats better not come by anytime soon." Mr. Sproat laughed and slapped his leg.

"You are quite a young lady, Deborah," he told her. "I do believe you'd run them off with their tail feathers dragging."

Back at her loom, she wondered what it would be like to disguise herself as a man. *Why not? If I marry, men decide everything. Women can own nothing.* Then, too, she'd heard that "Lord and Master" was the legal term for husband. Also, she knew many women worked long hours and had children to feed. Yet, Deborah noticed some luckier folks turned up their noses at these struggling women. It reminded her too much of her mother's life and how she'd had to give up her children. Deborah recalled how terrified she's been to be given away. She shook her head. *No, the desperate life is not for me.* Having served many years as a servant, Deborah knew she must find a way around the harsh English laws.

Still, the Thomases, and even her own mother (whom she seldom saw,) insisted that she find a man and marry. Deacon Thomas said, "Deborah you are 18 and you indenture soon fulfilled with us. You must find a man and marry him—or what will become of you?" They insisted she fulfill that social custom, like other girls. After all they noted, girls younger than she were already married and had children. "This is best for you, Deborah," they insisted.

Even the people at Deborah's church were saying she should marry. The minister gave a sermon called, "Choosing Time." He said "This is your choosing time. Girls should be choosing a husband. Boys should be choosing their life's work." Deborah slipped out of the service early to avoid people pressuring her to get married.

Deborah heard through the Thomases that her mother had found a man for her. "Well, I've heard of him," she said, and he's a drunkard. No, I certainly will not marry him." The Thomases suggested they invite him for Sunday dinner. But Deborah said, "Invite him if you will, but I will not be here." No one, it seemed understand her refusal to become some man's wife.

Deborah met other weavers while she worked at Sproat's loom. The village paper gave the time and place women gathered for weaving bees. Crowds of people came out to watch the expert weavers. Occasionally there would be a competition between two of the women, to see who wove the fastest and best. Mrs. Sproat judged the contest, and gave the homespun cloth to the soldiers who'd soon be off to Boston.

Often times the women wove a sprig of green and white, the evergreen rebellion emblem, into the cloth. As they worked, the women discussed various topics, including politics and philosophy. And to their surprise, people gathered to listen.

Deborah suggested a name for the group of weavers. "Let's call ourselves, 'The Daughters of Liberty.'" Everyone agreed to the name.

Captain Shaw and his militia men applauded the women for their homespun gifts. Deborah felt her face flush with pride during these moments. She also saw how the other women's faces shown, faces new to receiving recognition.

Soon some women in the village, asked Deborah if she'd weave clothes for their families. "We've seen your weaving, Deborah, and we can pay you a modest sum." And while Deborah continued to dream of a new Republic, she needed a steady job to live more freely on her own. She'd save the money, and see what else she could do to build a nest egg. It wasn't long before her answer came.

# Chapter IV

## Deborah the Teacher

As she ladled soup into the family's bowls for super, Deborah practically danced with excitement. But she kept silent until they'd settled into the quiet of the evening.

"I've good news," she told the Thomases as she darned the boys' socks. "The town council noticed I taught some of the neighbor's young children to read and write. Now, they want me to teach the older ones. I know they'd only hire me, because the former teacher is off fighting the British. I've been invited to stay with the Bourses for the next six months. Their house is at the edge of the school yard. The council will pay my bed and board," she explained, tripping over her own tongue in nervous excitement.

Mrs. Thomas corrected, "Deborah, you mean 'room and board.' You must speak correctly if you're going to teach."

"Yes, yes that's what I meant!" Deborah explained cheerily.

"Well, your indenture will soon draw to an end," the deacon explained. It will be good for you to find work to do. However, we want you to come back after school to help with the summer planting and fall harvest." Deborah's heart fell. That would be another year. Well, she decided, she'd just have to work day and night, and save her money until she could finally gain her freedom. Weaving and teaching... her path to independence!

Still, she had to laugh at the irony of it all. She was going to be a teacher, but she'd never been to school!

## A Ride to the Rafters

When school started, Deborah found herself in charge of a class of twenty children. Most were rowdy older boys. There were, however, two girls in school. Deborah wondered if the girls knew how fortunate they were.

On her desk lay a copy of *Gulliver's Travels*. The children loved to hear her read about the Lilliputians. Also on her desk was a Bible, a spelling book and the New England Primer. A long teacher's stick came with the desk. Deborah put the stick away. There wasn't a child who learned better with a whipping.

There were, however, a few unruly children. They'd run off some of the men teachers before her. To discipline a rambunctious boy, Deborah only asked one question, "Do you want a "ride to the rafters?" If the boy continued misbehaving, she'd toss a rope over one rafter. With the other end around the student's waist, she lifted the boy into the air. There in the air above his classmates, he'd fly, arms waving and feet kicking. Only when he promised to behave, did she let him down.

Deborah was glad to have work that paid, but she felt restless. "Teaching and weaving are fine for now," she mused, "but what then?" She tried to image a different future. Deborah searched her mind and heart for answers.

The next Saturday afternoon as she wove cloth for the Leonard family, Mr. Leonard told some startling news: General George Washington had called for a new kind of volunteer soldier.

Deborah dreamed of a new Republic. But she needed to work the year around to live free.

One evening as she cranked the butter churn, she told the Thomases, "The town council says I'm a good teacher, and they'd like for me to teach another term."

"Deborah, that's a kind offer, but we hoped you'd marry instead."

Deborah heard their serious tone, but she couldn't help herself. She laughed a merry laugh.

"Plenty of time for that," she said, not letting them dampen her joy. "I can teach in the day and weave at night." She passed around some hot bread to go with the fresh butter. Their faces fell. Mrs. Thomas tried again.

"Listen to this, Deborah. We have a letter from your mother. She wants you to meet a man from Plymouth. She thinks he'll be a good husband for you."

"Good husband?" she asked in surprise, slathering too much butter on her bread.

"Will you invite him over for Sunday dinner? I'll fry a couple of chickens," Mrs. Thomas said.

Deborah wanted to shake her head and shout, "No, no, no!" Instead, she spoke gently, "Let me think about it. Perhaps, in time...." She let them down easy. She hated disappointing the very people who raised her. She felt closer to them than her own family. "OK, everybody eat up while the bread's still warm," she said, passing around some strawberry jam..

## The Sound of Cannon

The next afternoon, Deborah climbed to the top of a hill on the farm where she heard a boom like thunder. Looking up she saw a clear sky. Then she knew... that was the sound of guns, of cannon. Her heart jumped with each blast, the *boom* echoing in her ears. *Must be trouble.*

Running to catch Bob, she jumped on the horse's back. She rode at a gallop to her mother's house in Plymouth. The frail woman stood outside, wringing her hands.

"My girl, a terrible, bloody battle is taking place near-by."

The mother and daughter stood in the doorway. The *boom-ba-boom* of cannons came closer. A cloud puffed over the treetops of the old apple orchard. Streaks of orange musket shot laced the pillowy smoke. Just then, her mother turned to her. "My daughter when will you marry? You are almost eighteen."

Deborah's mouth flew open then clamped shut. "Mother, how could...? Can't you see...?" *Had the whole world gone crazy*? "I can't think about that now, Mother. Your life and so many other lives are in danger." Deborah stepped back into the house. She took the musket off the mantel. Loading it she handed it to her mother. "Keep this by your side. I am riding to alert the militia."

She galloped through hidden back lanes to reach town. And as she rode, she thought back to May 20, 1776. when people at the town meeting in Middleborough voted for independence. The Continental Congress of the people governed them now—not King

George. *I was sixteen when the United States was born. Now I'm almost eighteen. My own freedom is about to be born.* She hoped.

Within weeks she helped Ransom and Jeremiah clean their guns and mold lead balls. She watched with sadness as they marched off to war. She felt like their sister, but she felt like their mother, too. She wanted to go with them, but knew she must keep her feelings hidden in her heart.

## Personal Independence

On Sundays, of her own choosing, Deborah went to The Baptist Church in Middleborough. She thought they were more open-minded than the Congregationalist. And on Saturdays and evenings, she worked on the loom at Sproat's Tavern. "This is the crossroads of the world. I'm in the thick of things here," she told Mr. Sproat.

She heard all the news and gossip about the war. The men talked freely as they played a game where a wooden ball is thrown to knock down pins. They called it skittles.

Back at her loom, Deborah enjoyed talking with people as they came to the inn. It helped pass the long hours. She was weaving when she thought again of disguising herself as a man. *Why not? If I marry, the man would only go off to war. I'd be left with children to feed on a good-for-nothing farm.*

Deborah noticed the wives who followed their husbands into war. Taking care of themselves and their children seemed impossible. Tagging along, they cooked and did laundry. Though it seemed women who stayed at home weren't much better off, no matter how hard they worked.

The women worked long hours trying to survive. Yet, Deborah noticed some luckier folks turned up their noses at them. It reminded her too much of her mother's life. *Such a desperate life isn't for me. My mother looked to a man for a living. You don't have to be a wizard to see the dangers. I care for my mother and her safety... but, I'm not going down that same dark road*, she vowed clutching her pillow.

## Women's Lives

"Trust thyself. Every heart vibrates to that iron string."
Ralph Waldo Emerson

Deborah became aware that English law wasn't good to the "fairer sex". Women could not own property. They legally owned nothing but the clothing they made. Nor could they vote in elections. Men decided everything. Lord and master was the legal term for husband.

A girl's father ruled her first, and then her husband. All her rights ended with marriage. She became her husband's property and lived to serve him. *Well… their lot is not for me*, Deborah pledged to herself.

The girl continued to educate herself through long nights of study. She wanted off society's lower rung.

When she visited the Thomases, she raised the hair on their heads. "If I marry, I'll never be able keep my money. That scares the wits out of me." Deacon Thomas, bewildered, shook his head at her remark. Then she added, "Why don't girls wake-up? Their freedom isn't real. It is an illusion." Her remarks made them gasp.

"Deborah, be glad for what you have," the Deacon scolded.

But after having served so many years as a servant, Deborah knew she must find a way around the harsh English laws.

In 1781 Washington had only a rag-tag army. The British were winning the battles. America reached out to the French and asked for help.

Cornwallis surrendered his army of redcoats at Yorktown. Everybody thought the war was over. General Washington said, "Don't be fooled. Those British will to keep on fighting." And he was right. Meanwhile, Deborah had her own battles to fight.

"Things will go well for you if you take this well-to-do man for a husband," her mother pleaded yet again.

"Mother we are at war. Besides, I can't marry a man I don't know, and don't love! The first time I saw him, he'd been drinking. The man is fool. Let his father buy him a slave," she fumed.

The Thomases and her mother threw up their hands. "I hope that means they know they can't change my mind. Besides, I know how to add. The sum total is, marriage to a drunkard is an unhappy business," she wrote in large letters in her diary.

In many ways, Deborah felt no different than other teenage girls. Many of them kept a diary, and dreamed of things to come. Though there was a difference. While other girls wrote of love and marriage, Deborah wrote about life and liberty.

# Chapter V

## General Washington Calls

In 1780 the war had begun to wind down. But General George Washington knew the war was far from over. He needed more fighting men. Without them, he feared the British would beat them yet.

He had a real problem. Volunteer soldiers only fought for three months. After that, they went back to farming. Washington needed men to sign up for three years. Washington announced to the people, "I've got to have soldiers who'll stay—until there are no British soldiers on this side of the ocean."

The young men of the colonies began to answer his plea. The new soldier became known as The Continental Soldier. General Washington called them, "America's first standing army."

Deborah knew about Washington's plea because everyone in the Middleborough was talking about it. One day as she worked at the loom at the inn, she overheard a recruiting officer talking to a young man. Deborah learned that more recruiters would be coming to Middleborough looking to enlist men for the Continental Army.

## Deborah's Disguise

At Sproat's Inn, Deborah heard about General Washington's plea. The Inn rang with recruiters for the Continental Army. As she wove cloth for uniforms, she overheard a recruiter say a bounty man was on his way to the village. He could be found at Israel Wood's house. New recruits would be paid handsomely, if they joined America's Army.

As the rain peppered down, Deborah sat dreaming on her bed. She thought about Washington's plea, and a plan began to form in her mind. She smiled to herself recalling the story her cousin, a sailor, Captain Simeon Sampson. He often told about his escape from his captors in the French and Indian War. It was simple he said, "I fooled them all by dressing as a woman." That's it, she thought, that's what I'll do. I will dress as a man.

Delighted with her plan, Deborah watched and listened to young men, noticed how they moved and talked. She secretly practiced when no one was about. She lowered her voice to a husky tone, then strode around kicking stones with her shoe.

At this time she worked as a weaver for the Leonard family. One evening while they were out, she decided to test a disguise. Deborah put on a suit belonging to Mr. Leonard. The girl wanted to see who she could fool. Deborah momentarily forgot about the common law that dressing as the opposite sex was a criminal act. She only thought about having fun.

At the tavern, she changed her laugh to a loud guffaw. *Passing as a man is risky, but I'm ready.* She mixed with the men as they drank their pints of stout.

Deborah's Pilgrim forefathers believed the water carried diseases, as it had in Europe. Every inn had its barrels of rum, gin and sometimes, tubs of punch. Ladies, however, never drank in public. That evening she returned to the Leonard's and quietly slipped Mr. Leonard's suit back into the trunk.

The very next night, Deborah began weaving a man's suit—her own coat, pants and vest. She made the vest loose, but wove a strip of wool to tightly bind her chest. "This is an order for a man in Plymouth," she told anyone who asked.

While some of her pupils paid her in Continental money, vegetables, and fruit, some of them gave her yards of cloth. She had put the cloth away waiting for the time when she'd need it. That cloth, plus the small amount she'd had time to weave for herself, made enough for a man's suit. Later she bought a hat, and ordered a pair of boots from the cobbler. *My old ruck sack, the cloth bag I carried over my shoulder, would have to do.*

Deborah began to feel anxious. *I've got to make this work. I have to play the part.* When her courage began to fail, she gave her voice a harder edge. *I'll put on manhood the way an actor puts on a costume.* Then time to test the disguise had come.

## The Test

Putting on her new suit with the new shoes and hat, Deborah decided to visit her mother. They'd not talked since the day they stood in the doorway, cannon booming.

Deborah knocked and her mother came to the door. "Hello, Mrs. Sampson, I'm Timothy Thayer from Carver. I was passing by and wondered if I might water my horse at your well."

Deborah could tell her mother didn't recognize her even as they talked face to face.

"Certainly, lad. Where are you bound?"

"Over to Plympton, to see a man about a cow." The horse finished drinking and Deborah jumped on his back. "Thank you, Ma'am. Your kindness is much appreciated."

They waved to each other as Deborah rode off.

Her disguised worked. She'd passed the test. Her own mother didn't recognize her!

*Now I'm ready.* Deborah went back to the Leonard's and waited for the right time. Within a week, a bounty man came to Middleborough. He wanted recruits for the Continental Army.

## A Youthful Mistake

Deborah felt encouraged by her success in fooling her mother. When alone, she practiced walking and talking like a man. She lowered her voice and growled in short sentences. As she walked, she took long strides. No more mincing daintily, she thought.

One evening, while the family was out, Deborah put on her disguise. *Let me see who else I can fool. This will be great fun*! In her enthusiasm Deborah forgot about the common law rule, although it clearly stated dressing as the opposite sex was a criminal act.

Putting on her man's suit Deborah walked to Israel Wood's house. She knew that an officer would be there to recruit men for the army

Going in, she looked about. By the fireplace Israel's gray-haired mother worked at the spinning wheel. Several eager young men talked and joked. One serious-faced youth talked with the recruiter who stood behind a table in the middle of the room. The bounty man looked at Deborah with a stern steady gaze. Her throat tightened—would her disguise work? She swallowed hard but kept her head up.

When her turn came, the recruiter beckoned by crooking his finger. Deborah stepped forward and deepened her voice. "I'm Timothy Thayer of Carver."

"So, lad," you're from out of town?" Deborah gave a solemn nod.

After a friendly chat with the recruiter, she signed the muster roll in a strong hand. He gave her the bounty in a leather pouch. Inside were four pieces of paper. On each piece were the words, "Thirty Shillings". Twenty shillings made a pound. Deborah almost laughed out loud. *Six pounds, I'm rich*! "The new company will form in a week or two," he told her.

Deborah kept her voice deep as she said goodnight and strode out. She hid her nerves by acting confident. But once out the door, she wondered, what if he runs out shouting, stop, imposter! When that didn't happen, she took a breath and relaxed. She'd been successful. Her fear turned to excitement.

I'll do what men do, she thought, go to the tavern and have a pint of stout to celebrate! The inn was crowded and noisy, the men jostling each other about. The atmosphere was heavy with the smell of tobacco smoke. She noticed that some of the men were none to steady on their feet. One man fell flat on his face. The crowd crowed, whooped and cheered their fallen comrade.

Success clouded Deborah's usually good judgment. The evening would come back to haunt her. She soon found herself in hot water.

At the tavern, Deborah had whooped-it-up with the other new recruits. There she had no trouble with her disguise. The barmaid treated her as if she was one of the men. But, mysteriously, word spread that "Timothy Thayer" behaved badly. Had Deborah overacted in her attempt to be taken as one of the rough and rowdy boys?

The next day, she taught her class as usual, thinking no one the wiser. However, things only seemed normal. Somehow, she'd drawn the suspicions of the people in her church. Soon the committee came knocking on her door.

## The Dead Giveaway

The elderly weaver, who saw Deborah sign the muster roll, had spoken out. "There's something strange about the Thayer recruit. That young man had a felon finger. And he held the pen like Deb the weaver."

The woman saw Deborah's felon finger—a stiff inflamed forefinger—common to weavers. The friction of twisting yarn caused a callused redness.

Upon hearing this, the church elders became suspicious. They went looking for Deborah at the school. They called her outside away from the eyes and ears of her students. One man pointed at her, "You have broken the law."

Deborah felt sick. Her stomach knotted. The power and freedom she felt, disappeared. Worry creased her brow. Deborah fretted her public shame would cause great humiliation for her mother. As a result her mother would be shunned by the town's people.

"It was only a lark," she tried to explain. Their faces turned red with anger. "We're taking your name off our rolls." The spokesman raised his fist as if to strike her, but they all turned their backs on her and walked out the door, their noses up in the air and their necks stiff.

Her thoughts tumbled over one another. She agonized over her run-in with the church. It had been the church of her choice. After a time, a strange calmness came over her. She had to act quickly— before the authorities came for her.

With all the deep hurt of a plan backfired, and the hostile response of her church, Deborah turned inward. There she searched for the strength to go on. From now on, she'd count only on herself to keep her hopes alive.

*If it hadn't been for Israel Wood's mother, I'd be in the army. But I can't look back. Gone is my life here—I must look to the future.* Destiny called and Deborah answered.

The minutes of the Middleborough First Baptist Church, September 3, 1782, reported: Deborah Sampson behaved unchristian like, dressing as a man, and left our parts in a sudden manner. It appeared that as several brethren talked to her before she went away, without obtaining satisfaction, concluded it is the Church's duty to withdraw her membership.

## Deborah's Departure

She waited until all were fast asleep. Pulling the suit from its hiding place, she put on the costume. Then, boots in hand, Deborah crept down the ladder from the loft. Midway, she paused fearful of discovery, but what she heard was only an ember tumbling in the fireplace. She quickly went out the door, closing it quietly behind her.

The next morning when Deborah was nowhere to be found, the Thomases told everyone, "She must have run away to relatives in Maine." Or that's what they thought because someone told them her father lived there.

"I always knew she'd come to no good—asking all those questions—and studying like she did. It wasn't right—her being a girl. I tried to tell her, but she wouldn't listen," Mrs. Thomas complained. Yes, they all agreed, Deborah's future looked bleak.

A tilted moon hung lop-sided in the night sky. She walked in its shadow some ten miles to Taunton. She'd have to choose another name. She couldn't use Timothy Thayer. *I know... I'll call myself Robert Shurtliff. He's one of the Sons of Liberty. I know enough about the family to answer questions—if I'm asked.*

Not having gone far, she pulled out her skinning knife. She hacked-off her hair to shoulder length. Then she buried the cuttings, and tucked the rest of her thick flaxen hair under her cap. "That's the way real soldiers do," she said to the lop-sided moon as she sped on.

As the morning sun rose on Taunton's green, she felt pangs of hunger. A smell of fresh baking bread filled the air. Glancing up she saw a man coming down the path. She ducked her head turning her face away. William Bennet from the next farm walked her way.

Making it to the bakery, she stepped inside. *Did he see me?* Panic gripped her. She didn't dare think what would happen if her plan failed. By law, she'd be a criminal for masquerading as a man. The thought of jail made her catch her breath. Though, right now, she was so hungry she felt faint... *surely they won't miss one of these stale hot cross buns*. With that she stuffed the roll into her mouth, and nearly choked getting it down. But before she set out, she grabbed more bread and stuffed it into her ruck sack. Though guilt overwhelmed her, and she left some of her hard earned money on the counter.

Then, she peered out the crack in the door, and looked up and down the path. She didn't see Bennet. Surely, if he'd seen her, he would have called to her, or followed her.

Taking no chances, Deborah walked quickly away from town. She jumped when the wind blew shadows across her path. Still, she saw no one else the whole day.

That night Deborah slept in the woods. A pile of leaves made a soft bed. She listened to a screech owl hoot in the darkness. Chill-bumps rose on her arms. The limbs of a chestnut tree scraped at the moon. She felt more alone than ever before. At last she fell into a troubled sleep.

With the sun up, the scary loneliness left her. Deborah rose, stretched and ate the left over bread. Soon, she found the path and struck out again.

As the girl walked, she thought about her friend who had read her palm. The woman did not know Deborah's plans. She'd told her, "You journey far. It will be successful. But there will be bad times, too. However, you'll be a good soldier... Why did I say a soldier? Only men are soldiers. Well, anyway, as for marriage, that's not for a long time."

Perhaps it will work out after all, she enthused. Deborah felt something like hope form inside. She walked faster, her spirits rising.

Hours of hiking made her thirsty and hungry. She stole drinks of milk from grazing cows. Getting a cow to stand still was difficult. "Sook cow, sook cow. Whoa, Bessie. Whoa girl," she soothed. Still hungry, she found a bed of tender curled fern buds and gobbled them down.

Once again, afraid she'd faint from hunger, she helped herself to a pie cooling on a porch rail. From time to time, she stopped at a farm and offered to chop wood for a meal. Those nights, she slept in the warmth and comfort of a barn.

# Chapter VI

## The Road Ahead

Deborah headed south through Rochester to New Bedford. She hoped to find someone else going to Army Headquarters. As she neared the town, her courage seemed to fail her. The girl trembled as she thought about trying to enlist again. *Will my masquerade succeed this time?*

Though she walked with an air of confidence on the road through town, she kept to the shadows. As she passed a group of people gathered in front of a stable, she overheard them talking. "A girl," one rough-looking man reported, "fooled the recruiter at Middleborough. She escaped from town bound for a hide-out, but if she's around here, we'll catch her—she won't get by us!"

The man's hard words struck her as if he'd thrown stones. Deborah quickened her pace, her breath coming in gasps.

When she saw a path leading off the road, Deborah walked toward the security of the woods and into the trees before she spotted a cave. She quickly scrambled up the hill and made her way inside. The musty smell of decaying leaves filled the small dim interior. But the shelter was out of the cool wind, and a good place to hide.

By now, the late April sleet slanted the gray sky and dotted the road below the cave. Rubbing her hands together to warm them, she searched her mind, looking for some way to calm her nerves. But fear of being captured and punished gripped her. She placed her hands over her thudding heart. She'd never been more terrified. Unable to hold back her tears, she sobbed. Finally, she lay back in the leaves and wiped her eyes. She could not go back, or beg for mercy from anyone, certainly not the strangers below. Still, undaunted, she knew she'd take her chances and try enlisting again.

For days she waited, gathering her courage. She moved about only under cover of darkness. Finally, she grew brave enough to leave the cave in daylight. But before noon her spirits dragged, and her confidence took a dive. She hadn't realized how hard it was to feed herself on the road. And she ached from sleeping in the damp, rock-strewn cave. Tramping along, her steps slowed as she began to feel sleepy, thirsty and hungry.

The girl tried to trap a rabbit, but that didn't work. Dejected, she sat down on a log, her head between her hands. Then in the stillness, she heard water. Walking on she found a deep clear creek, with a natural flowing well. She stooped and drank deeply from the crystal water as it splashed about her feet.

She wished she had her copper loop. Lying on the creek bank, she'd wait for a fish to swim by. She smiled to herself at how easy it had been. Dropping the loop around its head, all that was needed was a swift jerk upward. The lovely catfish, and the others she added to it, made for a good supper.

Here, now, she wasn't quick enough to catch the fish with her hands. Too weak from hunger, she lay down in a hemlock grove. The weary girl soon closed her eyes, and fell asleep on a soft circle of pine needles.

Suddenly she sat bolt upright. A rustling sound came from the thicket. *Maybe it's a bobcat or—a redcoat*! Deborah slipped away and hid behind a clump of thick bushes. To her relief, a ground squirrel popped into view. Whew! She whistled in relief. When her heart stopped hammering, knew she must calm herself for what lay ahead. What could she do, she asked herself, now that she was being hunted and in all kinds of trouble?

Various thoughts came to her. Then she asked herself a question: What would her cousin Simeon Sampson do? He always had ingenious ways of getting out of trouble. Now, he was a famous naval captain.

That was it! Maybe, she couldn't become a sailor, but perhaps she could find work as a cabin boy on a privateer. She'd heard stories how these vessels were used to raid English war ships. She laughed right out loud. No one would think to look for a runaway girl on a ship. That night she set out for New Bedford's dock and a fleet of sailing ships.

## The Ship's Captain

Standing on the wharf at New Bedford Deborah watched the sailors bustling about the ships. Occasionally, she heard them shout to one another, their voices floating over the water. They didn't appear interested in hunting down runaways. The dark bulk of the whaling ships see-sawed in the water. Deborah picked out the graceful privateers that bobbed gracefully among them.

Her stomach growled and she felt the need for meat and bread. She left the docks and went to find an inn away from town, but close by the water.

Entering the inn, Deborah made her way through a crowd of rough, boisterous men. She stepped up the bar to order food. "Yes, lad, what'll you be havin'?" asked a tired-looking woman with a soiled red kerchief in her hair.

Deborah found a small table in the corner and began to wolf down sausage and chowder-soaked biscuits. She drew the attention of an old sailor who came up. He grinned, "Young laddie, you're putting that tack away like it's your last meal. You'd better slow down or you'll make yourself sick." He slapped her on the back which had the unfortunate result of making her belch. The sailor threw back his head and howled with glee.

Deborah waved her hand, as if to say, I'll be fine, while she kept chewing. Swallowing at last, she asked, "Do you know of a captain who's in need of a cabin boy?"

"I caution you, lad, some captains are fearsome hard on their cabin boys. One boy I knew disappeared altogether," he growled, cocking his head and fixing her with a hard stare. "Some of those captains turn into brutes, once they're out of sight of land. Though they act upright and respectable when they're ashore, he volunteered. They're even seen taking tea with rich widows."

"Uhhh, well, thanks for the tip," she said, "I'll watch my step."

*He means well*, Deborah concluded, as she walked out the door, but those captains can't be all bad. I have to give it a go anyway, she realized, crossing her fingers.

Deborah picked out the ship with the most activity on deck, and started up the gangplank. "Would you be looking for a cabin boy?"

she called to the imposing figure watching her from the rail. The burly man nodded.

"You served a captain before?" he queried her.

"No, Sir, but I learn quick."

"Come aboard, lad," he invited, gesturing with his hand big as a bear's paw.

With a rolling gait that came from years walking on a tilting deck, the captain showed her a filthy ship. He told her the duties of a cabin boy: "You'll shave me, empty the slops, hold a pot for the queasy—vomit—, fix my food, and assist the ship's surgeon." They walked on a bit and he pointed, "Up here is where you'll sleep."

Deborah looked but saw only a twelve inch wide wooden shelf. That's a bed, she wondered? That moldy, rocky, old cave would be better than this. She nodded as if enthused, but kept her feelings to herself.

The girl did not like the captain or the job, or his revolting smell from downwind. Her stomach gave a lurch imagining working for him in close quarters. And then there was a matter of having to sleep on the shelf. She had to get away without making him suspicious. She knew sometimes men and boys were shanghaied —kidnapped— taken by force to work on sailing ships. And perhaps, here, she'd innocently walked into a trap.

"I have to go back and pay for my room at the inn, she lied to the captain. "I'll be back before you sail," she promised.

"Ye better be, if ye know what's good for ye," the captain threatened. The gleam in his eyes underlined Deborah's suspicions.

She walked back down the gangplank and moved fast in the direction of the inn. Deborah sped along; afraid the crazy captain might send someone looking for her. Once out of sight of the ship, she tramped on northwest to the town of Bellingham. She couldn't help steal a look over her shoulder from time-to-time; afraid she might be followed.

Within a mile of Bellingham, a farmer with horse and wagon stopped. "Looking for a ride, youngster?" Throwing caution to the wind, and to ease her aching feet, Deborah gratefully jumped into the hay.

At Bellingham she leaped from the wagon, and brushed off her suit. She heard a drum beat in the distance. "They're drumming up recruits for General Washington," the farmer informed her. "But they won't take you. Without a beard, they'll think you're only a baby," he laughed uproariously, slapping his leg.

Deborah set off walking toward the sound of the drum. There she saw a pasture where the recruiters stood behind makeshift tables. She immediately shoved her hand with its felon finger in her pants pocket. Stepping up to the recruiter's table, she swaggered with a sureness she did not feel. *Will I be found out? This is my only chance.*

"God help me," she prayed.

The officer looked Deborah up and down, as if taking her measure. He must have thought she had the makings of a soldier. She thought he looked strong, but not mean. "Well, young man, you want to be a soldier?"

"Yes, Sir. A Continental Soldier." She gave her name as Robert Shurtliff.

"I'm going to list you for the quota at Uxbridge. But you muster in at Worchester. You can find your way there with these other fellows. He picked up a leather bag. "This has your bounty money, boy."

Though desperate for money, Deborah didn't want to appear overly eager. She waited until the recruiter handed the bag to her. Money meant food and shelter. Her stomach twisted as if pleading for her to hurry.

"Who's in charge?" she asked coolly.

"General Paterson's in charge of the Fourth Massachusetts, Colonel Shepherd's Regiment. You'll be in Captain Webb's company."

Gathering with the other volunteers, Deborah walked with the men the three miles to Worchester. They seemed to be a spirited, good-hearted group, talking as they went. Deborah felt excited about seeing her regiment for the first time.

## A Continental Soldier

(1782 to 1784)

A drill sergeant from West Point met the recruits at the Worchester Inn. It was his job, he sourly noted, to make soldiers out of them. They were the last batch of three-year men he would have to train, and glad of it, he said with down-turned mouth. With that, he motioned his aides to pass out fusees—wooden friction matches—knapsacks and cartridge boxes.

What she saw next made Deborah's eyes pop. She was given a splendid blue uniform coat. Then one of the aids handed her a waistcoat, breeches, stockings, boots and a cap. The new recruit could hardly keep from whooping with glee. A beautiful uniform and it was all hers. She took a deep breath and swelled with pride. Then, looking around at the others, she blanched. The men were taking off their clothes! Deborah thought fast. Picking up the uniform she walked nonchalantly to the stairs.

"Where do you think you're going?" growled the sergeant.

"Upstairs. My brother's here to take my suit. I promised it to him."

"Bring your brother back and sign him up, then he can have a new *blue* suit," laughed one of the men. The new soldiers hawed and hollered their approval.

In an empty room upstairs Deborah took off her smelly filthy man's suit, and stuffed it into a trunk. Next she quickly splashed herself with water from a pitcher and basin. Oh, how refreshing. She breathed deeply. Following that, she re-wrapped her chest with the length of cloth. Deborah's flat-chested boyish form returned.

She tenderly touched the uniform coat, and sighed with pleasure. The coat, itself, was a thing of beauty. She took it up and put on her new stiff uniform. Standing tall she looked into the mirror. The image staring back at her was that of a man.

The sight of herself in full military uniform made her catch her breath. The effect was stunning. The French-made uniform's blue coat was lined with white. The epaulets—fringed straps—topped the shoulders. A cord of white outlined the arms and pockets. The white waistcoat and breeches topped black half boots.

Deborah admired the hat most of all. Made of white leather, it was tall with a chin strap. She noticed how the cap's red-tipped, rosette plume glowed in the light from the window. This makes me look real "cocky" she mused.

"Private Robert Shurtliff, Continental Soldier," she barked. No gesture, no word must give away her secret. Her disguise must be perfect.

Deborah took a few moments to practice her strut and swagger before the mirror. Then she turned and bolted down the stairs to join her company.

Now, more than ever, she understood the importance every man look like the others. The uniforms gave the impression they were all alike. They were *all* men—an illusion Deborah was counting on.

## Marching from Boston to New York

The new uniform saw hard wear on the two-week march in 1782. The regiment left Worcester and went north toward New York. Their destination was West Point, the Army's military academy. On the way, they skirted Boston. Deborah thought about the time she and the Deacon dropped off corn for the people. She hoped their action had done some good—and the corn was taken to hungry people.

It was agony marching double-time ten miles a day for 14 days. Each soldier carried thirty pound packs. The new heavy wool uniform rubbed Deborah's skin raw in places. New boots pinched and blistered the recruit's feet, until she limped. One night in camp Deborah took off her boots and realized she was in danger of losing the nails on her big toes. They were bruised and starting to turn black. Her feet had almost frozen in the blast of unseasonably cold weather. The ground seemed to either ooze freezing mud or was rock-hard like ice.

With the rest of the company, Deborah suffered in the chill wind, and soaking, thunder storms. At night some of the men slept in their clothes. Deborah slept in her damp uniform. This did not cause suspicion, because some of the men slept in their uniforms, too.

The weary soldiers didn't mind, she noticed, crawling into a sour-smelling tent and dropping off to sleep. Deborah heard that others slept in their breeches for a reason. One soldier asserted if he didn't sleep in his breeches, "somebody might steal 'em.".

"Besides," another man chimed in, "I'm not going to fight Brits dressed in my drawers—not with them dressed in those fancy red coats."

On the worst days when they trudged uphill over rugged terrain, the soldier feared falling over in exhaustion. She knew she was strong, but this tested her mettle. Other soldiers struggled too. But she noticed Richard keeping an eye on her. Once when she stumbled and almost went down on one knee, he lifted her up. "We're buddies," he said, punching her arm.

Deborah felt a warm glow when she looked at him. He was handsome and friendly. She felt her face redden, but Richard had turned away. She was glad he had not seen her response to his touch. Deborah felt surprised she had become interested and curious about Richard.

The soldier had to will herself to keep the pace and not fall behind. She tried to keep Richard out of her mind, but it was difficult as he marched near her. They were both struggling to keep going. Toward the end of the two week march, Deborah wondered if she was really strong enough to make it to West Point.

Her hands were blistered and bruised. Opening and closing them, with the stiffness of the dead, was very painful.

Deborah almost lost heart. But at her lowest point, she heard a voice in her head. She recognized it, at once, as the voice of her namesake, Deborah, from the Bible. The same voice that had come in her dreams, now urged her to go on. I will if I have to die trying, she answered.

At last she saw the sparkling waters in the Hudson River Valley. She stood on a tall ridge looking down. She'd made it. Pride mixed with the bone-tired weariness within her.

Below her stretched a valley of huts and tents. She estimated there must be enough military housing for thousands. West Point stretched at length along the water and back to the far tree line. The man next to her said their regiment would be among the best equipped, clothed, fed and housed, of any of Washington's troops.

General George Washington let it be known the Hudson River Valley was a strategic area, and that the war would be won or lost there. He'd set his hopes on West Point's troops, that they would capture that area, and truly win the war for American independence.

Just as the recruiter at Bellingham had told her, Deborah became a part of Colonel Shepherd's Fourth Massachusetts Regiment. She was in Captain Webb's Company.

The men were given a flintlock musket, a knapsack, a cartridge box and thirty lead balls. Other equipment included a fusil, (steel for a tinderbox), wooden canteen, bayonet—knife fit to the end of a gun—flint, and powder.

The soldiers kept busy cleaning their guns and doing drill exercises. Deborah also worked to remove the soil from her uniform. By being meticulous in dress and appearance, she hoped to avoid any close inspections.

Once each morning the company drilled on the parade grounds. At four o'clock they drilled again. Deborah strove to move with a dignified bearing. She carried herself tall and straight, and hoped she looked like the perfect soldier. It wasn't long before she heard about her officers' good report:

"Robert Shurtliff shows excellent bearing, endurance, alertness, and has outstanding proficiency in drill. He is agile, strong, and demonstrates leadership. He learns quickly and with spirit."

Being praised by her superior officers amazed and thrilled Deborah. Acting the role of soldier paid off. Deborah, along with Richard, was among those the officers chose for the Light Infantry— an undeniable honor. One thing was sure, no one would look for a girl in an elite army corps, or so she fervently hoped.

## A Letter Home

By May, Deborah began feeling guilty. She'd left home without a word to anyone. The young soldier decided to write her mother.

Deborah chose her words carefully. She wanted to let her mother know she was well, without revealing her whereabouts.

*"Dear Esteemed Parent: I am in a large but well regulated family. My work is somewhat different. It is more intense than at the Thomases or in Middleborough. But I feel it is equally as good. My supervisors are upstanding people. They demand the best conduct. I have had many useful lessons in life. Still, I have many more to learn."*

Before Deborah continued, she paused. How could she say what she wanted without giving herself away? Still, the girl felt the need to reassure her mother that she was safe. Then she continued, *"Be not too much troubled. I try to take virtue and wisdom as my model."*

Pausing again, she searched for the words which would not give away her location. Chewing on her lip, she squinted her eyes for a moment thinking. She decided to give only a hint as to her locale.

*"I live in a lovely residence along the banks of a river. And I am well. May peace come to our nation, so I may return to the embrace of a parent whom I love."*

*Your affectionate daughter,*
*Deborah Sampson*

# Chapter VII

## A Light Infantryman

All through her service Deborah never let her guard down. The fear of being caught stayed on her mind. If the British captured her she'd be punished as a traitor. And if caught by American troops... well, the public humiliation was too much to contemplate.

Ever vigilant, Deborah did not rough-house with the other soldiers. She never let anyone put his arms around her shoulders. Two other things she did not participate in—sick call and getting vaccinations. When it came to bathing, she made sure she got up first each morning to take the required swim. As to her personal needs, she went into the woods.

Meanwhile, Deborah continued to fit her girl's figure into the army issued uniform. Wrapping her chest with length of wool, she let her waist go free. Being used to a corset, it didn't much matter. It was a small price to pay, she felt, for being able to serve as a soldier.

## General Washington's Charge

"The fate of unborn millions will now depend, under God, on the courage and conduct of this army." General George Washington.

The government wanted the army to enlist better men. They didn't want drifters and adventurers. To this end, the army's "Blue Book" ordered officers to "inspect into the dress of the men. See that their clothes are clean and put on properly. Their faces must be washed and clean; hair combed; equipment ready; and everything about them in order."

The officer's were impressed with Deborah's "spit and polish," and her willing attitude. The elite Light Infantrymen were chosen because they'd be quick and courageous in dangerous situations. As a member of this select group, Deborah would soon be near the enemy line and on picket (watch) duty. Officers told Light Infantrymen their main duty would be to go on missions to scout out the enemy, and encounter them.

Deborah's commander warned, "The redcoats keep terrorizing the colonists, even though the war slows down. For you, however, the war is only beginning. The eyes of the world are on you."

The soldier knew as a light infantryman, she'd soon see action. Almost unbearable tension continued to build in Deborah. There was the stress of hiding her identity, and, at the same time preparing for the coming battles. Nerves became her enemy, and she being incredibly anxious, stopped eating. Deborah was always in the mess line, however, though the sight of food made her queasy. The secret soldier only pretended to eat, moving the food around her plate. Feigning fullness, she shared her meal with the other soldiers who were only too glad to take it. Anxiety and fearful thoughts kept her awake at night. She lay wide-eyed staring at the ceiling rafters. She often did not sleep until first light shown through the cracks in the door.

In the hut, which she'd help build, she was in close contact with the men in her company. Deborah never spooned for warmth, and slept apart. The soldier had to endure the sounds of men's snoring, chuffing and thrashing about in their sleep.

In the mornings, she went through the motions feeling numb and weary. Yet, no one stopped her and asked why she stumbled. Though a friendly comrade, Richard Snow, told her she looked ghostly pale. Other than that, no one seemed to notice.

To build her confidence, she told herself, over and over, to breathe slow and deep. And eat... something. She must have strength. Deborah began to choke down food at meals. The girl followed her own instructions until, at last, a measure of calm and confidence returned.

Deborah would have to think of reasons to be away. Find ways to get out of quarters as much as possible. To this end, she volunteered for patrol.

Within a month, her unit began patrolling along the border of "No Man's Land." On one particular day, there being no enemy to encounter, they sang, *Yankee Doodle*, as they marched. She laughed recalling how they'd sung it around the supper table at the

Thomases. They'd made it America's song. Her spirits soared. Then, without warning, a shot rang out. They all dove for cover leaving the song echoing in mid-air.

## Life as a Warrior

All the while, Deborah resisted calling attention to herself. Unless, it was to volunteer for a patrol. This took her away from camp—lessened the chance of discovery. No one would question her identity, if she stayed gone on patrol to raid the enemy!

From the very beginning, it was her habit to avoid close quarters. All the soldiers slept in their clothes. This helped her keep up her disguise. No one saw the band of wool that compressed her chest. When she couldn't stand the smell any longer, she risk a quick dip in a pond or stream. Though in cold weather she endured and wiped off when she could. The girl never, ever, answered sick call. That was too risky. A doctor would discover her disguise. Always, she worked out her illnesses alone.

There were other precautions. At no time did she "horse around" with the men. She always found other work to do around camp. This kept her away from arm wrestling, or some other foolishness. Skillfully Deborah maneuvered and kept on the move. Though, sometimes, she bemoaned the anxiety of masquerading.

She wanted to go back home and be done with all the fears, the hiding who she was. Still at times she was glad to be gone. The Thomases are good people. They took her in as their servant when my mother couldn't take care of her. But she'd earned her freedom. And she *really* wanted to be free—though easier, she thought, if I were a man.

Deborah sighed. The Thomases and her mother would never change their minds. They'd never understood her need to learn and to live her own life. They steadfastly demanded she find a man and marry. Although Deborah listened to the adults around her, she had taught herself to read and write—and she'd read some colonial law. A wife belonged to her husband. Like having another master—being a servant. *Fiddle de de. I'm not doing that again.*

She smiled to herself—well she'd found a good family now, the army. The army fed, clothed and treated her as a worthy individual.

Deborah was helping the colonies, as well as setting her own course in the world.

Difficulty and danger followed the Light Infantrymen everywhere. The men and one lone girl, fought, dug trenches, constructed forts, and built bridges over deep rivers. Deborah and her comrades even found themselves cutting and setting timbers for a chapel at West Point.

But for all their efforts, the news was not good. Cornwall's surrender at Yorktown, in October of 1781 did not end the fighting. Battles continued as Washington said they would. While peace talks went on in Paris in March of 1782, both armies were starving.

Now, risky patrols and skirmishes—hit and run fighting—took most of Deborah's unit's time. But starving soldiers did not fight well. The battles took another turn. Both sides competed to find animals, hay, vegetables, cheese and milk. Survival, and victory, depended on it.

The two opposing armies were on either side of "No Man's Land," an area thirty miles wide. The Light Infantrymen camped in the New York Highlands. On the other side were the British in New York. By now, Deborah was hardened in body, strong, but still tender of heart.

America and her army were worn down by the war. The biggest problem was lack of food. Neither side had enough.

Deborah saw that the colonists did all they could to help them. They gave cattle, horses and food to the soldiers. Meanwhile, the British raided the Whigs—colonists loyal to America—for food and cattle. The redcoats boldly took whatever they needed from the Americans. Likewise, The Light Infantrymen rode out to take all they could take from the Tories—those loyal to the Crown. As America's original country "bandits," the famished men, on both sides, did not stop to ask ownership of, say, a hen. Snatching the bird up it soon would be roasting over the fire.

Both armies sent out scouting parties. "Send me as a scout," Deborah told her commander. The soldier soon gained the reputation as a clever, courageous scout. Whenever she volunteered for duty, she was quickly accepted. All the officers wanted "Bobby" in their raiding parties. She knew staying in camp, made discovery more likely. Staying gone was safest, but she also knew the chances of being killed were greater.

## Cowboys vs. the Skinners

British Colonel Delancy led The Westchester Light Horse Battalion, nicknamed the "Damned Cowboys". They excelled in raiding colonial homes and farms. They worked in the night, stealing everything they could find. They herded off horses and cows. The pigs gave them more trouble.

Deborah rode with the "Skinners" who scraped off the Tories (British sympathizers) in the countryside. She excelled at, and enjoyed, stealing hams out of smokehouses, as she'd learned to do back at the Thomases, egged on by Ransom and Jeremiah.

Whenever Deborah was asked to go out on a mounted raiding party, she jumped at the chance. On this particular night the "Skinners," rode from the Highland along Post Road toward New York. "Hey," one horseman yelled, "let's catch the Colonel and then fill our bellies with cheese and ham." A cheer went up from the men.

The Skinners knew a cave where the Cowboys stored an abundance of food. The men smacked their lips as they rode dreaming of making off with jars of honey, butter, and cheese—and hams from the enemy's smokehouse. Deborah's mouth watered as they rode.

Under cover of darkness, they were happy to find Delancy and his cowboys inside a farmer's house eating supper. This was going to be easy, Deborah thought. A guard stood watch, but soon they bound and gagged him. The leader motioned for Deborah to make her move.

She squirmed into the smokehouse through a window. The inside was as black as the inside of her cap. She struck a light from her tinder box. (A box with flint and steel for striking a spark.) The lid acted as a candle holder.

Knowing time was running out, she quickly got a spark and lit the candle. With a swift slash of her knife, the hams came tumbling down. She threw them out the window, to the waiting arms of the Skinners.

"O.K. Private Shurtliff, set this tic of straw on fire. Throw it in the smokehouse. That'll get 'em out here on the run," came the leader's whisper. "Then we'll get Delancy."

After setting the fire, she jumped on her horse. Racing off, Deborah heard a shout from the farm house. A bullet whizzed over her head. It struck the pine tree in front of her. She turned to look back. At that instant, she felt a searing pain in her leg. She'd been hit.

The Skinners made a line in a row of trees. "Let 'em fire a couple of rounds and then return fire," the leader shouted.

She felt the boot on her right foot fill with blood. In her thigh, she found where the ball entered. Deborah felt as if she was going to pass out, but she willed herself to stay conscious.

When a fellow soldier approached and asked to look at the wound, she brushed him off saying, "It's only a scratch." She dismounted, and gave her horse to the soldier. But with every step, pain howled through her head like a wave crashing on stone.

As the skirmish went on, Deborah crawled off to find a place to hide. A hole, covered with vines, hid her well. Lighting a candle from her tinder box, the soldier put the knife into the flame. The lead ball had to come out for she feared lead poisoning. The young woman drank a ration of brandy. Staring at the torn flesh of her leg, she drew a ragged breath. Some of the amber liquid she saved, knowing it would be needed again.

The soldier braced herself against the dirt wall of the hideout. She held a hickory stick between her teeth. Biting into the wood, she dug at the wound with the knife. *Aaaarrrrgh* sounded from her throat. Finally the musket ball came out. Her tears fell into the blood spurting from the wound. Deborah poured the rest of the brandy into the wound to sterilize it. Getting a cloth from her pack, she mopped at the blood. At last, she stopped the flow, bound the wound, and fell over exhausted.

Sometime in the night, Deborah cried out waking herself. Water gurgled nearby and she dragged herself to it. A natural cistern flowed in a mossy hollow. At the water the soldier fell face first into it, gulping. She'd never been so thirsty. Deborah filled her canteen, and then washed herself and the bandages while thinking how good a piece of ham would taste at that moment.

After four days, the secret soldier made her way at night along the Hudson to Tarrytown. There she found her scouting party.

"Bobby, Bobby, we won!" they shouted.

"Tell me everything!" she yelled, over their whoops and hollers.

"Colonel Sproat and his boys ran off the "Damned Cowboys!"

"Hooray for the Skinners!" Deborah shouted.

All the while thinking about Sproat, the young woman remembered how in Middleborough the owner of the inn joked about her joining the army. Deborah was glad not to be present when he showed up. He might've recognized her, and said, "Deborah, girl, what are you doing here?" That would have been the end for her.

The young soldier slipped away when the camp doctor came to her area. She had to prevent his poking at her wound. One look and she was sure to be sent packing, straight to jail.

## Richard Snow

Weeks after being shot, the secret soldier was sent on a mission with her unit. "Go as far into enemy territory as possible," the Captain ordered. The thought of trying to march with her wounded leg, made Deborah's head swim.

Tramping along, the soldier tried to ignore the jarring pain in her leg. The man in front of her, Richard Snow, struggled too. The next instant he hit the ground, twisting in agony. "Company, halt," Lieutenant Gilbert called. He made his way back to the fallen soldier. Deborah spoke up.

"Sir, let me take Private Snow to a farm house. Get him some aid. Then I'll catch up with the troops," she offered, thinking, if I don't faint first.

"Very well, Private Shurtliff. Keep an eye out—this is Tory country. A lot of the citizens around here are Tory's, loyal King's Men. Don't take any chances."

"What have I done?" she wondered as their patrol marched away.

Deborah helped Richard to a nearby farmhouse. The owner, Mr. Van Tassel, a known Tory, opened the door. Her heart sank at the angry expression on his face.

"We need your help, Sir."

Van Tassel made no move to let them in. "Why should I open my house to you?" he growled.

"It isn't for me... it's for this man. We'd be grateful if he could rest here." Finally, the glowering farmer let them in.

"Don't show your faces, or I'll lock you in the attic," he threatened.

Deborah eyed the ladder to the attic. Did she have the strength left to get them up there?

Stooping, she put Richard over her shoulder and started up the ladder. Every few rungs, the soldier stopped, breathing heavily. Sweat poured from her face. The searing pain in her leg caused her to gasp for air. After Van Tassel had turned away, his bright-eyed daughter had slipped in. Deborah could not see her, but heard her encouraging voice as she helped by boosting them up until they reached the top.

The exhausted soldier laid Richard on a small pile of dirty straw. He was barely breathing. Then sitting down on the attic floor, she waited for she knew not what. Rats could be heard scratching in the corner. After a time, the young soldier heard someone start up the ladder. *Friend or enemy?*

The Tory's daughter stood in the opening holding a large bowl. "I'm Sara Van Tassel. He looks like he could use some soup," she said pointing to Richard.

"Thank you, young lady. You're more help than you know," the secret soldier told her.

That night, loud voices floated up from the room below. Through cracks in the floor boards, she saw Van Tassel drinking with some redcoats. Deborah held her breath. What if Richard cries out in pain? That'll be the end of them both....

The next evening when Sara brought soup, she looked sadly at Richard. "He doesn't look any better.... I also brought him up some fresh water from the well. You can have some too," she smiled.

"I haven't given up on him," Deborah told her, "Though he lost consciousness today."

"Maybe he'll be better tomorrow," Sara said, looking hopeful as she turned to leave.

Deborah took that opportunity to take off her jacket and chest binder. She dipped a cloth into a bowl of water. It'd been many days since the young woman had a chance to bathe.

To her horror, she heard Richard speak. She tried to cover herself, but it was too late.

He whispered, but she heard him clearly. "Thank you—whoever you are—for your tender woman's kindness to me."

"I won't leave you," Deborah promised, still gripping the cloth to her chest.

That night Richard feebly held out his arms to her and spoke tenderly. For Deborah it was the first words of love she'd heard from a man. They clung together through the night, as if they both knew what the morrow would bring.

Before dawn, Richard died. Deborah closed his lids over blue eyes, and touched his lips with her finger tips. She said a prayer and then wrapped him in his field blanket. Dipping her hand into the water bowl, Deborah wiped the perspiration from his face, brushing his dark hair from his forehead. For long minutes, the young woman looked at his hands before taking them into her own, thinking of his gentle caresses. Then, holding him in her arms, Deborah crooned to him as she sat rocking on the hard cold floor of the attic.

Deborah took the few personal effects Richard had given her, a scribbled bible verse, a favored grandmother's gold locket, one she'd given him for luck as he'd marched off to war, and a letter to his parents. Deborah put them in her haversack, except the locket. Richard made Deborah promise she'd keep the locket to remember him by. The soldier knew she must keep it hidden, so there would be no questions. After the war the young woman would find his parents, and give them Richard's few things. Deborah would tell them what a fine, brave son they had.

With Richard dead, Deborah knew she must escape as soon as possible—if what she'd heard from the room below was any indication of Van Tassel's plans for the wounded soldier and his buddy. But the soldier waited until Sara climbed the ladder to see about them.

Van Tassel's daughter, her eyes filling with tears, said she'd see to Richard's burial. Deborah's heart swelled with gratitude for the young girl who'd helped them, and who would do this last thing for them.

When the girl left, and night came on, Deborah climbed out the window and down the heavy vines that grew up the wall. The secret soldier vowed she'd keep Richard in her heart forever, and that she'd never forget the courage and compassion of young Sara.

# Chapter VIII

## Bagging a General

Limping along, it took the soldier almost a week to catch up with her patrol. Finally, with tips from Whig farmers along the way, she tracked the soldiers to Newport, Rhode Island. She explained to her officer about the death of Richard Snow and where he was buried. "You're lucky to get out alive Bobby. Van Tassel is an infamous Tory."

But within the week the soldiers were full of talk about their next skirmish. "We're out to bag ol' General Prescott," the men told her. "He's an old bird who's holding the whole Rhode Island colony captive. People everywhere are upset about what's happened. They're like prisoners in their own homes."

The first night they set out to capture Prescott, Deborah was amazed to see five American whale-boats, captured by the British, lined up on the beach. The only light came from a bit of moon. The orb looked no bigger than a nail clipping.

The men tied burlap around their oars to soften the sound. They knotted a rag to the top of a pole in the first boat. Deborah looked hard trying to keep that flag in sight. They stayed in the shadows. As Deborah's boat passed near the guard, she heard, "All's well." He never looked their way.

Deborah and the boatmen watched for a signal from the shore. Then the soldier helped pull their boat up on the sand. Running with the others in the darkness, soon they'd knocked down a cabin door. Deborah was amazed to see the General in his bed. Startled awake, he obviously had not expected their visit. After they'd quickly bound and gagged him, he wasn't much trouble. Then off they went, dragging the barefooted man through the sand, his nightshirt flapping in the breeze. Tossing him into the boat, Deborah and her comrades were away before the British missed their general.

## Tight Quarters

The Light Infantrymen worked as carpenters in the coldest part of the winter. With them Deborah helped build a huge hall at West Point. They also built themselves one-room cabins. The soldiers liked these quarters better than their freezing tents.

Their cabins were big enough for six to eight soldiers. Each hut had a fire-place and a dirt floor. Crowded together, they cooked, ate, slept, told stories and joked. Deborah, fearing discovery, did not like the tight quarters.

The secret soldier stayed outdoors as much as she could. Working on the hall and other carpentry tasks kept her away from the cabin during the day. At night Deborah had to take her chances.

One afternoon, while she worked on the hall, a huge log fell from the building, and took her with it. The soldier crashed to the ground injuring her nose and an ankle. Shaking it off, Deborah told the others working with her she didn't need to see the doctor. The young woman couldn't help but limp from the fall, though she kept a smile on her face. But smiling hurt too, though she tried not to look pained.

Then she heard something that caused her spirits to greatly improve. It was rumored the general needed an aide. Deborah knew aides served food and drink. Also they cleaned the general's boots and helped him dress. Maybe this could be the chance she'd been waiting for. If the young woman were chosen as the general's assistant, this would free her from staying in the cabin. Private Shurtliff waited until she saw her Captain, "I'd like to be an aide," she told him.

"Don't know who decides those things Bobby, but I'll pass the word along," he told her.

It rained on the morning of April 16, 1782. In fact it had been raining for days. The wet weather made slop out of the drill field. It was on that day the general sent for Private Sampson.

Deborah hurried to wash her hands and face, and clean her uniform. She spit-polished her boots until she could see her face in them. But the effort proved useless even though the soldier picked her way carefully across the drill field. Mud splattered her boots, and Deborah knew General Paterson would not tolerate that. She'd been warned the man simply did not accept excuses.

Nonetheless, wading on, she came to the backdoor of headquarters. Then Private Shurtliff heard the staff officer yell, "Off with those boots! The general won't have you tracking in mud."

After her boots were cleaned, Deborah followed the officer down the hall. Her heart pounded in her chest. The private had only seen the general from a distance as he sat on his horse. To think about being in the same room with him was, frankly, terrifying.

The young woman paused at the open door. Deborah swallowed hard over the lump in her throat. She saw the proud profile of the general as he sat at his desk by the window. The soldier entered the room and saluted. The general motioned for her to sit down.

"I've a good report on you, Private Shurtliff. You're an excellent soldier. Do you think you'll be as good an orderly? Can you serve a table of officers and shave my face?"

"Yes, Sir," Deborah answered in a strong voice which belied her inner tremor.

"I want you to help my wife and family as well. Are you willing?"

"Yes, Sir. An honor Sir."

"In that case, I believe you'll do. From now on, you're my personal orderly. You'll have your own room here at headquarters. I'll see to it that you are given a good horse and fine equipment."

It came to Deborah she'd no longer have to sleep in the hut, or a moldy tent, or on a straw mat on the damp ground. She'd sleep on a feather bed! When the men in the cabin heard of her good fortune, they'd be green with envy. The young woman's apprehension lifted; she didn't have to hang around the cabin with the men!

The general kept Deborah busy carrying messages on horseback to far places. Almost immediately, the general and the private worked well together. She felt he trusted her, and that he acted, unknowingly, as her protector. No one would look for a woman on General Paterson's staff. Deborah jumped up and clicked her heels.

As the general's aide, Deborah accompanied Paterson to all his meetings. Consequently, the young private met many people important to the military. She liked General Robert Howe, a rice planter from South Carolina. The young private also admired the fine junior officers who came up through the ranks like her former officer, Lieutenant Benjamin Gilbert.

As always, Deborah watched and listened. She saw first hand how powerful men conducted business with Congress. The soldier paid attention and noticed the way the military men drew up petitions—put names on a list—and how they made alliances. Alongside General Paterson, she watched as he signed important papers and documents.

Deborah took it all in. The soldier absorbed how men took power and used power. But she also learned what not to do. Word in the ranks was that some of the officers fought duels, drank heavily and bragged. Private Shurtliff recalled her own misbehavior while disguised as Timothy Thayer. The young woman knew she'd never again act like those would-be gentlemen officers.

And it became obvious to her that General Paterson's troops loved him. And Deborah felt he'd won her over too. In 1783, the general was thirty-eight years old, and the young woman twenty-two. Paterson became like a father to the "fatherless" soldier. He became the father the young woman never had. That old familiar black knot in her stomach disappeared when he was around. Deborah felt safer than before, and lucky to be his aide. In her mind, the young soldier called him, "My old friend."

Still, the emotional burden of her disguise came and went. To Deborah her life seemed a strange one of fear and relaxation. Still, her time as aide to General Paterson was the highlight of her life, to that point. Meanwhile, the general created changes in his own life.

In 1783, he sent a message to Congress. "I want to move my headquarters to the red house at West Point." Congress gave the general what he wanted. They held him in high esteem.

"Private Shurtliff, I want you to move with my family to our new home." Deborah could not believe her good luck.

The general, his family and Deborah lived in the red house for only a month, when the general gave them bad news, "General George Washington ordered me to take my troops to Philadelphia—as fast as I can. The soldiers there are angry and may revolt."

One of Deborah's friends, Lieutenant Gilbert, sent a message to the general, "The soldiers are rioting. They were sent home after the war with empty pockets."

In June, 1783, the war ended for good. At first the soldiers cheered— then they booed. They'd been sent home without a penny. Even General George Washington received nothing but thanks.

"All the money is gone. It's been spent for the war. There's nothing to give the soldiers," congress said. Yet, they wanted General Paterson's troops to protect them from what they felt was an upcoming mutiny. The members were concerned for their own personal safely.

That very day, General Paterson gave Private Shurtliff her orders. "Follow me in four days. Ride with the gentlemen officers. You will find our troops camped on a hill outside the city."

Reaching Philadelphia, the general reported back that General Washington had put down the riot. Still, the city reeled from the impact. The first day, after Deborah arrived, Paterson sent her into the city on business. She kept her eyes open. The young woman thrilled to be in the heart of American Independence. Deborah shook her head. *Can this be me? Can this be true?* The soldier wondered. The determination and spirit of independence Deborah noted all around her, took her breath away.

## Disaster in Philadelphia

Within days, Deborah heard reports in the general's office that a sickness roamed the city. Brain fever killed soldiers and citizens, alike. This news scared her.

On the second day, the general sent her to Independence Hall with a message. Deborah completed the mission and came out of the hall, where she stood in front of the Liberty Bell. The young private reached out and touched the sacred bell with her fingertip.

Suddenly, she felt unsteady. The soldier sat down on the grass. Then, to her horror, she threw up. Vomit stained the front of the soldier's fine uniform. She tried to stand, but passed out crumpling to the ground.

Moments later when she came to, the soldier found herself on a stretcher. Two military men, unknown to her, carried the confused and ill soldier through the streets Philadelphia. Her skin felt on fire. "Make way. Make way," they shouted pushing through the crowd. Deborah tried to get up.

"Put me down, I tell you. Put me down!"

"Sorry, lad, we can't do that. We're taking you to the army hospital. The captain says you probably got the fever. The boys back in camp don't want it. Too many dead already," he added cheerily.

Deborah tried to get up again, but fell back. She heard the fife and drums and then felt panic. *Is my corps leaving me?*

Entering the overcrowded hospital, the men put Deborah down on the floor among the dead and dying. "Please take me out of here. I can't breathe," she pleaded to a doctor passing by.

"That's not possible, soldier. We've got epidemics of small pox, measles and typhoid in this city. You'd only give it to others. We'll take care of you here."

When Deborah saw a nurse, she struggled up on one elbow. "Nurse, I beg you, take me some place where I can get some air." The Director of Nurses, Mary Parker, overheard the soldier's plea.

Parker gave instructions to the nurse, "There's room in the third floor loft, nurse. Only a minute ago, two men died. Take the soldier up there." Hearing those words, Deborah passed out again.

Sometime after midnight, she opened her eyes. The room seemed to weave back and forth. A candle sputtered on the floor. Two men stood over her in a heated argument.

"Stop yelling. You're gonna raise the dead," one insisted.

"Well, I get his coat and breeches," the louder one bellowed.

"No, I get them this time. You got the boots off the last one we buried."

*They fight over my uniform. They think I'm...dead!* Deborah realized with a jolt. The young woman tried to make a sound. But only a gurgle escaped from her throat. Shocked, the two grave diggers jumped back.

"Call Doc Binney (Bee-nay). This one's not kicked the bucket yet."

"Suits me—but I get the next one."

## Doctor Binney

By the time Dr. Binney climbed panting up to the loft, Deborah was barely breathing. The doctor felt for a pulse at her neck frantically searching for the throb.

"Does the heart beat?" he muttered. Deborah felt him push back her soldier's coat and unbutton the shirt. "What's this?" he wondered aloud, seeing a man's chest bound in cloth. The doctor expertly cut through the material. He gasped at what he saw, "Great God in heaven! Can this be?"

Running to the ladder he called down. "Matron Parker, come with me. A soldier's returned from the dead!" As she came up the ladder nearer him, he whispered, "She's a girl!"

The doctor and matron worked feverishly together to revive Deborah. When he could not find a heart beat with his ear trumpet, Doctor Binney raised the soldier's head. He lifted brandy to her lips. Deborah gasped, choked, and sputtered, and tried to rise up.

"Lie back, my dear. You've been through a hard time. You also have a bad case of pneumonia," Matron Parker informed her.

The doctor and his assistant looked at each other. "What are we going to do?" she asked.

His head down, the doctor stood a moment in silence before he answered, "Nothing until I can think this through," he replied in a stunned voice. They stood in silence. Then he said, "If the officers find out, things will go hard for her. Let me take her to my house. I've turned three of my rooms into hospital rooms."

"She won't be discovered there," the woman nodded.

"Cover her. Then call the lads to take her over to the house."

Deborah's drew a ragged breath and lost consciousness again.

When the soldier came to, she found herself in a clean nightshirt, and lay on fresh ironed sheets. Feeling her forehead with her palm, there was no fever. But now, whoever put her in this room must know her secret.

Deborah cringed. *How can I explain myself to the person who brought me here?*

Shortly, Deborah heard footsteps, and the door to the room burst open. To her surprise, both a doctor and his assistant came to her bedside. The soldier prepared herself for a barrage of angry accusations. Instead, to her relief, both strangers smiled warmly. The pair did not question or shame her. First the doctor and then the woman introduced themselves. They pointed out her uniform, cleaned and mended, which lay on a chair by the bed. And with the uniform there was a new linen binder.

Doctor Binney said, "I want you to stay with my family until you are well. Then, when you're strong, you can return to your unit." He paused, and then asked, "Do you mind giving me your name?"

Deborah, head down, answered the doctor. "My name is Deborah Sampson. I became Private Bobby Shurtliff when I joined the army." Then, looking up, she went on, "Thank you, Sir. I am forever in your debt."

He waved her thanks aside, but his eyes held a smile. Deborah knew Dr. Binney would keep her secret.

When Deborah recovered sufficiently and could walk, she dressed in her uniform and at the appointed time, went into Binney's dining room. She'd been extended an invitation to dine with the Doctor and his family. His wife and three lively daughters greeted her.

"Do come in, Private Shurtliff," Madam Binney welcomed, moving aside as the young daughters rushed forward, "It's Bobby," they chorused, hugging her about the knees.

The time came when Deborah had a chance to talk to the doctor in private. The soldier again tried to express her thanks. "You saved me from the grave, a ruined career, and a bleak future," she said, reaching out to shake his hand.

Doctor Binney asked Deborah about her life in the army. She told him about the battles and how she had been wounded. She talked about how she loved being General Paterson's aide. "I have a great affection for him and his family. He is a good and kind family man, like you," she beamed. Deborah saw she had pleased him as the doctor beamed back at her.

Binney listened closely to Deborah. Now and then, he asked a question. "Your secret is safe with me—however, I must send a letter to General Paterson. He needs to know your whereabouts."

The doctor's three little girls, hung on Private Bobby Shurtliff's every word. She read to them, and taught them new games to play by the fire.

"Our daddy's always bringing sick soldiers home, but you're our favorite," they enthused. Deborah basked in the family's warmth for her, and felt thankful for it.

When she felt well enough to travel, Doctor Binney decided it was time for the soldier to "look to a new day." He gave her a letter. "Take this to General Paterson. He's returned to West Point with the troops." He paused. "You're an amazing young woman. I wish you every success. When you can, write me a letter, tell me about your life."

The doctor took Deborah to the stage coach. He paid the driver to take her to West Point. They shook hands and then Deborah climbed aboard the stage. As it drove away, Deborah looked back and waved farewell. She knew this would be a turning point. She put her hands to her face and felt the heat, not knowing if she felt thrilled or terrified about the road ahead.

As the stage rolled and bumped along, the soldier's eyes were drawn to the leather pouch that lay on the seat across from her. She wondered what Doctor Binney had written to the general, and finally admitted to herself; perhaps she *did* have an idea about its contents.

The young soldier recalled her days as the general's *aide-de-camp*. He'd chosen her because he liked her quiet bravery. Now, she prayed he'd give her a military pardon—if Binney had, in fact, revealed her secret.

As the stage creaked and lurched along, Deborah took the sealed letter out of its leather pouch, and held it in her hand. A keen feeling told her it informed the general who she really was. She fought back the tears. Her breath caught in her throat as she struggled to regain composure. The soldier knew General Paterson recently court-martialed two Pennsylvania mutineers who were then given the death penalty. She swallowed hard. Would she be whipped, drummed out? What? she wondered.

Misery turned to near panic. *It's all over—I'm done for.* Deborah gazed forlornly out the window, her mind conjuring up pictures of a dark future. Then as her stage rolled to the water and started into the Hudson River, a terrible storm stuck. The sky turned black; roiling water began to fill the floor of the stage. The driver, struggling with the team and the swaying, bucking stage, was unable to save her rucksack that fell with a huge splash into the river. Deborah felt stricken as she saw all her possessions float away.

Deborah's valuables lost, the young woman thought of a tempting idea: she could toss the letter into the tide with the rest. It would surely look like an accident considering the situation. She raised her arm, preparing to fling the tell-tale letter into the drink, but something stopped her. She reconsidered destroying the letter. Deborah did not wish to fail in her last duty as a Continental Soldier. She could not, would not, fail to deliver a message meant for General Paterson. Her honor was at stake—even if it meant her death.

As if her pledge had delivered them from the strong current, the straining horses slowly drew the stage out of the water and onto land.

# Chapter IX

## West Point and General Shepherd

As Deborah's stage pulled up before the Great Hall at West Point, the men of the light corps shouted when they saw her. "We thought you were dead, Bobby. Hooray, Hooray for Bobby Shurtluff!" Their warm welcome boosted the soldier's courage for what lay ahead. A courier stepped through the crowd and handed her a message from the general. In it, he stated he wished to see Private Shurtluff as soon as he arrived.

Leaving the stage and her comrades, the letter case in her hand, the soldier set off for the red house on the hill to meet with General Paterson. She thought about the day they met, and swallowed a lump in her throat. Straightening her shoulders and taking a deep breath, Deborah tried to control her fears. The soldier tried to smooth her rumpled uniform, and wiped at her still damp boots. It was crucial she present herself with no flaws in either demeanor or dress. As for her secret flaws, Deborah agonized, those would be revealed soon enough.

"You're looking well, Private Shurtliff." The general smiled broadly at her as he motioned her to sit down.

Before she complied, Deborah handed the general the letter. "For you, Sir." Without so much as a glance, he tossed the letter onto his desk. The general settled down in an armchair across from her. Without further ado, he said "Now, we need to get to work. I've a list of errands for you to run. Return to my office as soon as you've put your room in order—it is the same one you had before you left for Philadelphia. With an officious clearing his throat, he continued, "There is much to do this day."

Deborah rose, snapped a salute. When she reached her room, the young woman closed the door, fell on the bed and struggled to control her emotions. Still, a tear slid from each eye.

Within minutes, someone knocked on the door. "Private Shurtliff, General Paterson wants to see you in his office at once." Deborah struggled to pull herself together. She wiped her tears and blew her nose. Taking a deep breath she braced herself for what would surely follow. Her knees felt weak as she made her way back down the hall.

## Explaining Things to General Paterson

As Deborah stepped into the general's office, sweat channeled in rivulets down her spine. General Paterson sat ram-rod straight. Only his watered eyes belied his emotions. "You've been an excellent and faithful aide." A long pause followed as the general looked out the window. Deborah hoped he'd finished speaking. But he focused his eye again on her and continued. "I only ask... does your uniform hide a feminine form?" Deborah choked from the knot tightening her throat. Gripping the arms of the chair she tried to maintain control. She struggled to breathe.

The young woman and the general looked at one another. Moments passed. It was, she thought, as if they were seeing each other for the first time. The great man held her eyes in a steady gaze, though he looked as flushed as Deborah had ever seen him.

"Your heart and spirit I admire. You've always acted with bravery and faithfulness. Although I will not dishonor or punish you, I will not allow this charade to continue; you can't wear the uniform of The Light Infantryman—or any military uniform. I am turning you over to my wife and daughters—they'll find you proper feminine clothing."

"Sir, I... " She stopped when he held up his hand.

He tensed and leaned forward in his chair. In a quieter tone he inquired, "Miss Sampson, I must ask... why did you do it?"

Deborah momentarily hesitated then found her tongue. "Thank you, Sir, for your mercy. To answer your question... I only wanted to see the world and serve my country. I wanted to be free to do so. There was no other way for a woman."

Drawing a deep breath, she went on. "I've always behaved well. You can ask any of The Light Infantrymen. No one but you and Doctor Binney know who I am."

Deborah grew uneasy under the general's stern gaze. She wanted to run away from the scene. An awkward silence sat between them. Looking out the window and seeing her fellow soldiers at work, she turned back to him, blurting out, "With your permission, Sir, I'd like to be dismissed. I see the fellows outside need a hand chopping wood."

"Miss Sampson, you cannot go on with your masquerade— successful though it's been."

The young woman searched his face for signs of betrayal. He went on, "Don't worry. I'll not tell the men."

"Sir, I'd rather face cannon fire than go back to my former life."

The general cleared his throat and stood up. "Now, now. We'll have none of that. My wife will help you. You must make a change of clothing before you start for home."

Upon hearing the news, a startled Mrs. Paterson put her hands to her face and sank into a chair. "So, your real name is Deborah? Is our beloved Bobby, really a...? Her fingers now fidgeted on the chair arm. Well, ah... Deborah it is then."

"Yes, Ma'am. The general said you'd help me find a dress. Deborah kept her eyes down. She thought she'd die from embarrassment.

"Heavens to Betsy, if that doesn't beat all," Mrs. Paterson said, as she sat back fanning herself. "Well, come on then." Mrs. Paterson stood up. "I have a few things in my trunk that might fit."

She helped the soldier into one of her own dresses, then Mrs. Paterson set about washing and curling Deborah's thick wheat-colored hair, that she'd worn pulled back in a queue. The young woman had never braved the heat of a curling iron. She cringed when it came too close to her ear.

"Sit still," Mrs. Paterson scolded.

Finally when Deborah's dress and hair met Mrs. Paterson's approval, they stood before the mirror. They both looked amazed. The older woman's eyes twinkled. "Let's see if we can fool old Colonel Jackson. He's one of your commanding officers, true?"

The two women let General Paterson in on their plan. He sent for Colonel Jackson. Soon Jackson sat in their parlor waiting to meet, as they told him, a lovely young woman.

As Deborah entered, Colonel Jackson stood. He reached for her hand and kissed the tips of her fingers. She remembered to make a curtsy. "I am charmed to meet such a beautiful lady," he said. The two sat with the Patersons, and made polite talk as they sipped tea.

A satisfied smile played on Mrs. Paterson's lips. Deborah sensed the lady was pleased she could pass for who she really was.

Then there was a break in the talk. The girl's thoughts raced. *Oh no, she's not ...*

"You've met Deborah before, Colonel," cooed Mrs. Paterson. The man looked blank. "Surely you remember meeting her," she went on sweetly. "She wore the uniform of The Light Infantryman."

"I don't understand." Then an amazed look crossed his face as it dawned on him. Startled, the colonel bolted up jostling the tea table. The china cups clattered and tipped over in their saucers, sloshing the costly tea on the floor. Flustered, he excused himself with a slight bow.

The general held up a hand. "Hold on, Colonel Jackson. Forgive us our little trick. We only just learned of Private Shurtliff's secret. I'll see to it she leaves the army in good standing. May I count on you to do the same?" The colonel his voice shaking with anger managed a tight-lipped,

"Yes, Sir."

The general continued, "I talked to the men of the fourth regiment. To my surprise some of the men had recently gotten word of your disguise. To a man they gave good reports. They said you did your duties with courage, fearlessness and great control. They were amazed with your determination. They can't believe you're a girl.

## Victory

On September 3, 1783, a peace treaty was signed. The war was over. Deborah left the general's office discharge papers in her hand on that very day. They held the signatures of both the general and the colonel. She looked around. The sky was bluer, and the bird song sweeter than she ever remembered. America had won her independence, and she had played a small part in the victory.

## Going Home
(1784 to 1797)

Deborah left the red house at West Point carrying a small box. In it were her uniform and honorable discharge papers.

She felt odd in a pink dress, bonnet and slippers. A lace ruffle scratched her neck. The shoes pinched worse than the waist cincher. And how could she hitch a ride wearing such a getup? Deborah dug at the bonnet ribbons that cut into her flesh under her chin.

Deborah felt it'd be a lot easier traveling in men's clothing—and safer too. The young woman wished she'd had the man's suit she'd woven before she left home. The new civilian didn't fancy having to jump onto a hay wagon in the restrictive clothes. Besides, Deborah knew a woman traveling alone might come to harm. Then, as she strode forward she tripped on the flowing skirt and staggered before regaining her balance.

As soon as she found a stone wall, she stepped behind it, and took off the traveling outfit. Untying the waist cincher at her back proved to be a challenge. Finally, she took out her knife and reached behind her cutting the strings.

"Ahhh," she sighed in relief.

Deborah put on her uniform and boots. The elegant attire she placed back in the uniform box. "These are so pretty. Maybe they'll be of use some day," she mused aloud. But Deborah couldn't help feeling a little guilty. After all, she'd promised the Patersons to wear the clothes they gave her for her journey home.

The new civilian now understood what the other soldiers said about going home—it was difficult. Already she felt nervous. Not only did it mean the end of a shining military career, but she had to face her mother. The young woman knew her mother would be angry with her for walking off without a word. Deborah only hoped her mother remembered she'd written her a letter.

She worried, and wondered if she could undo the damage her going away must have caused. How would she be received? Would her mother welcome back an unruly daughter? And what did her relatives think of her? Deborah especially fretted about John Bradford, a relative of her mother's, who was governor of Massachusetts's Plymouth Colony.

Deborah shook off the questions. She had to get moving. She walked straight on to her Uncle Nathaniel's house in Plymouth, although it took her several days and nights, where she knew her mother now lived.

The girl was saddened when a stranger answered her knock on the door. "Mr. Nathaniel Bradford died," he said. "Mistress Sampson moved to live with her cousin over in Sharon. Are you the cousin's son, Ephraim, from the army?"

Deborah nodded, then turned and walked away—her nerve gone. The thought of facing her mother brought tears to her eyes. "I can't do it," she muttered.

She walked along, kicking at stones in the road. What would she do now? Then it dawned on her. Her Aunt Alice and Uncle Waters lived in Stoughton, 40 miles to the northwest. The walk was a long one, and she'd have to find somewhere to sleep along the way. Deborah wasn't concerned; she was used to a hearty military life, and could adapt to almost any circumstance. She didn't give the trek a second thought. Uncle Waters was a real patriot and her aunt had a sweet personality. The thought of seeing them again caused Deborah to feel hopeful, and she quickened her pace.

Deborah's uncle and aunt welcomed her with open arms. "We'll invite our friends over. They'd like to talk to a real by-golly soldier girl!" The dress, hat and slippers stayed in the box.

For weeks Deborah entertained people with her stories. Each time she finished, they'd say, "Tell more, girl soldier." People could not get enough of her recounting her escapades.

After a while, Deborah began to feel restless. "I need some real work to do," she told her uncle. "I've enjoyed sitting by the fire and talking. But the day has come for me to go."

Although she admitted to herself, life was much better now that she didn't have to act a part. Still, being "a curiosity" wasn't enough for the former soldier.

Uncle Waters told her about a farmer in Sharon who needed a hired hand. Did she think she could do the work? "Ha", Deborah laughed. "If there's one thing I know how to do, it's work." Deborah readied herself to leave the next morning. But not before that she helped prepare breakfast and washed the dishes.

"Thank you for all your kindness," she told her aunt and uncle. "You've given me a real welcome back." There were hugs all around.

"Come back, anytime, Girl," they called, as she started up the road.

## The In-Between Time

Deborah arrived in Sharon after the long hike. She met a couple walking down the path and from force of habit, tipped her cap to the lady, and asked them directions to Ned Billings' farm. The returning soldier sat on the steps of an old stone church to rest a bit, before she started out again. Deborah wore her regimentals—her soldier's clothes, to be dressed for farm work in barn and field. A dress would only have gotten in the way.

When she arrived at the farm she stepped up on the porch of the house, but before she could knock, stout farmer Billings barreled out the door, almost slamming into her.

Deborah stepped back hiding a smile at the near collision, and at the bumbling but energetic man. Clearing her throat she introduced herself. "I'm Deborah Sampson from Middleborough. I was in the war. I'm out of the army now and looking for work."

This startling news made farmer Billings blink, but he quickly regained his composure.

"I don't care what you did or why. There's too much work here for one old man. I need another strong back to work this farm. Do you know farm work?" He eyed her closely.

"Yes, Sir. I can handle any of the chores you set me to." The farmer hired her on the spot. Billings showed her to a small room which had been added onto the back of the house. It was sparsely furnished with a small iron cot. But to the young woman a room all her own was a welcomed sight.

"My wife has passed, but I can manage to feed myself. Can you look after your own needs?" Deborah assured him that she could and not only that, she'd help him with acquiring provisions.

"I'm pretty good with a squirrel gun. And there's no reason we can't have plenty of venison to eat." Billings face lit up as he smiled a toothy grin.

"Then we ought to get on right well."

Deborah passed the winter and early spring as a farm laborer. A neighboring farmer, Benjamin Gannett, often came by to talk to Billings. Deborah overheard them exchanging ideas about crops and weather. At times, one or the other spoke to Deborah about her work.

Before long, the former soldier realized Benjamin stopped by, but only to talk to her. He'd heard from Billings, she'd fought in the War of Revolution. Deborah liked Benjamin's quiet way. There were times he gave her a hand with the farm chores, so they could have more time to talk. When there was need for more firewood, they'd make short work of the wood pile, swinging their axes together with wood chips flying.

Deborah liked Benjamin, and the work on the farm was good enough, but she kept thinking about her mother. Something in her felt an urgent need to visit her and to make things right between them. This thought tormented her for some months, until she gave Billings notice that she'd be moving on.

Soon after, on a Sunday, she walked the 20 miles from the farm into Sharon. Arriving there mid-afternoon, she knocked on her mother's door. Her cousin Hannah opened it, and immediately recognized her. She jumped up and down hugging Deborah. "Come on in, and welcome stranger!"

Deborah saw her mother with Hannah's baby on her lap. Deborah's mother stared at her daughter as she stood in the doorway. "Nehemiah is that you? My brother's come to visit!"

"Mother, this isn't Nehemiah, he has passed away. Don't you remember? This is Deborah," Hannah said, wrapping her arms around her cousin's neck.

"I don't believe it," her mother said, squinting up with dimming eyes.

"Yes, it's me, Mother," Deborah said, but her mother still didn't believe her.

"Oh, you're fooling me, Nehemiah. Come sit and have some tea."

Deborah motioned to her cousin. They went behind a partition in the room. Deborah took the crushed dress, bonnet and slippers out of her rucksack.

Standing before her mother in Mrs. Paterson's dress, she curtsied. Her mother gasped.

"It that you my runaway girl?" Then the woman's amazed expression turned to a frown. She scolded Deborah, "Come and hug your old mother. But promise never to put on men's breeches again."

Deborah smiled and gave her mother a warm embrace.

In the days following, Deborah's mother said she didn't know if she could ever get over her daughter's unladylike behavior. "You have behaved in a scandalous way, daughter."

But Deborah didn't give up. Everyday she helped her mother in some way seeing to her comfort. Deborah worked tirelessly at winning back her mother's affection. The young woman hoped in time they would makeup. But her mother continually urged Deborah to make changes—to behave more ladylike. Deborah smiled and patted her mother's arm. "We'll see," she said.

The cousin's family and the neighbors were happy the female soldier had come back to them. Still, they also wanted her to make some changes. "You must ride sidesaddle. After all," they told her, "that's what ladies do."

Deborah smiled, "We'll see," she said.

It was best she not tell them about riding with the "Skinners". They'd faint dead away to hear about the raiding parties. Or that dresses, corsets and sidesaddles were very much a bother.

Deborah found other women in the neighborhood quite distant. They were not pleased with the young woman having been a soldier. Still, at times, she saw their eyes light up with admiration. She understood why they dared not follow her example.

At the same time, she knew none of the soldiers had yet received pay for their war service, including General George Washington. She needed to make a living. Deborah thought she'd best return to teaching. Also she wanted to help provide for her mother. The young woman applied for a position in the school at Sharon, and was hired. She found a room in the home of one of her young students. Deborah threw herself wholeheartedly in teaching.

# Chapter X

## A Suitor Comes Calling

One afternoon as Deborah stood in the schoolhouse door dismissing her students, Benjamin Gannett rode up driving a new black buggy. Hitching his horse at the gate, he waved to her and strode up the walk. At the door he stood with his hat in his hand. "Hello, Miss Sampson. Do you remember me, Benjamin Gannett?"

"Indeed I do," she said and felt herself blush.

She saw he'd trimmed his dark hair and mustache. His trousers and shirt were clean and pressed. *Why, he's come courting.* Suddenly, she felt shy.

"May I take you home, Miss Sampson?" he asked. She noticed him looking at her—with the bluest of eyes.

"It isn't far," she replied, "I easily walk to the house where I'm rooming. But, I'd welcome a ride because my shoes pinch," she confessed laughing.

The farmer took Deborah's hand and assisted her into the carriage. As they rode, an embarrassed silence grew between them until Benjamin broke the ice. He began to talk to her about his experiences in the Sharon Militia. "But I didn't get to see much of the war. I wanted to fight, but my parents are old and needed me on the farm. I served on the Committee of Safety, though. I kept an eye out for any suspicious enemy activity. We tried to do our part by giving cattle and grain to the army."

Deborah only half listened as something else took her attention. "That's a fine spirited stallion pulling this buggy."

"My first love is fast horses. Do you like him?"

Deborah nodded. "Oh, yes, indeed."

"I used to call him 'King', but because the British have a King, I changed his name to 'Star.' There's a star shape on his forehead—you'll notice—and there's stars on our new flag."

"Well, enough about me and my horse. Tell me about your time in the war. I want to hear more about the fighting." Benjamin listened to Deborah, his eyes wide, as she told him about riding with the Skinners, building the chapel at West Point, and capturing the General.

On another fine spring day, Benjamin came by the school house. He rode one saddle horse and led Star. "I want to show you the farm," he told her. "Will you ride with me?"

Fearless, Deborah jumped astride the stallion's back, her skirts flying. "He's a beauty," she yelled to Benjamin over the pounding of hooves. She leaned forward urging the horse on. The horses and riders flew over the meadow. Deborah knew Benjamin loved spirited horses—although she'd begun to suspect, he loved her more.

While at the farm, Benjamin introduced Deborah to his father, Benjamin Sr. The elder Gannett was a well-known patriot, supporter of the Continental Army, and a wealthy farmer. Deborah immediately felt that Benjamin's father liked her, and was intrigued she'd served the country in the war.

Following one of their wild races, Deborah and Benjamin led their horses to drink at a near-by stream while they sat together on the bank under a flowering tree. Solemn, twisting his hat in his hands, Benjamin asked Deborah to marry him. Then, after he'd proposed, added a bit breathlessly, "I love spirited horses, but I love you a whole lot more!"

Deborah did not give Benjamin an immediate answer. She patted his hand and gave him a light peck on the cheek, and told him her answer would be forthcoming—she didn't say when. His forlorn look tugged at her heart.

Deborah had long feared her break with the church would come back to haunt her. But within a few months a committee from the church came to call. Probably, she suspicioned, they were asked by Benjamin's father to repair the breach between them and the former soldier. Deborah, they said, had been forgiven for her former indiscretions. The spokesman, staring down his nose at her, said they understood she'd mended her ways and was now behaving "like a lady should." Yet for their talk, no one actually invited her back to church.

Geared as Deborah was to being independent and resourceful, the young woman felt content being single. She thought back to how much her mother and the Thomases had pressured her to marry. Yet none of the candidates for matrimony seemed even slightly of interest to her, one being a drunkard and the other shiftless. And although she'd heard some folks called her a "masterless woman," she did not know how life would work out as Benjamin's wife. *Would I be able to settle down to a life of domesticity?*

As their relationship grew, Deborah knew Benjamin loved her for herself. She felt she did not have to disguise who she really was. This was a great relief for her, to be accepted for herself. And the pair was delighted to find they had ancestors in common, John and Priscilla Alden.

They talked about how on the Aldens' wedding trip, while John walked beside Priscilla, she sat gracefully on the back of an ox, flowers in her hair. Benjamin assured Deborah, "My love, you don't want to be wed sitting on an ox. I will give you the great prancing stallion, Star." If Deborah had any doubts before, she now felt she loved the gentle farmer, but still hesitated to set a wedding date. She had grown to enjoy living in an independent fashion, and did not know if she could risk her future for any man.

Deborah suspected Benjamin had talked to his father because it wasn't long before Gannett, Sr. did something that nudged Deborah to consider setting the date.

The young woman was breathless when widower Gannett presented her with a beautiful dress. The gown formerly belonged to his first wife and he'd had it altered for Deborah. It fit except the hem had to be let down three inches.

The woman's doubts began to fade as she traced her finger tips over the fine, off-white, imported, English cotton fabric. The gorgeous dress was printed with blue pinecones, seashells and flowers. The ankle length gown featured three-quarter length sleeves with ruffles, and a square of fine linen called a fichu—a triangular drape or shawl worn around the shoulders and tied in front. It was modern in design and Deborah could not resist it. Then to her amazement, Benjamin's father promised them a 45 acre farm if they were to marry.

And although the generous gifts made Deborah feel overwhelmingly lavished upon, what really made up her mind to marry was this: she felt their admiration, and knew for the first time acceptance without a disguise. And it wasn't long before Deborah decided to become Benjamin's wife.

Their wedding announcement came out in the Sharon newspaper. Almost two years from the day I signed up for the army, Benjamin and I will marry, Deborah mused. She read it aloud to Benjamin, "Deborah Sampson of Middleborough and Benjamin Gannett of Sharon will marry on April 7, 1784 at the home of Mr. Gannett's father in Sharon, Massachusetts."

Benjamin asked her to never change, and Deborah sensed that even after they were married, he'd be pleased with her the way she was—outgoing, opinionated and with a strong will. She felt some security for the first time in her life. The former soldier looked forward to their working their own farm together.

And as before, Deborah kept up with the news, and knew what went on in politics. She also knew what was being gossiped about in the village. As it turned out, some people still talked against her. Though some forgave her "fall into rough company," and changed their tune, saying, "She's all womanly gentleness and peacefulness." Yet, no one invited her to tea.

## Wedded Life

Two years after they married, a son was born to Deborah and Benjamin. They named him Earl Bradford after Deborah's Pilgrim ancestor, William Bradford, the first governor of the Plymouth Colony. Polly (Mary) came three years later, and then little Patience arrived.

Deborah also found room for an orphaned infant, Susanna Shepherd. The baby whose mother died giving birth and whose father could not care for her alone. Deborah adopted the child and raised her as one of their own. "I've always felt like an orphan myself, and would have adopted all the war's orphans," she told Patience Payson, who was an older orphan and household helper of the Gannett Sr. family. She was such a favorite of the children and the Gannetts', they named their third child after her.

So the former soldier found her days busy with farm and family. The children were young and required a lot of care and attention. "It seems one of them is forever falling into and out of things, the pond, the fireplace—including the butter churn," she lamented. "This makes more work as I must then bath the sticky child and feed the contents to the pig."

But Deborah found she could not work as she'd done before, and it distressed her to put in fewer hours in the field and the kitchen. Her leg plagued her with pain from her war wound. Consequently, Benjamin had to deal with most of the farm work without any help. They could, now, barely support themselves and the children. She became miserably unhappy as she crippled about doing her many chores and duties.

About the same time, she picked up the newspaper and read by candle light that the soldiers of Massachusetts were currently being paid for their war service. This news came after a long weary day of mowing hay. But Deborah knew she had proof of service, and hoped her former officers would vouch for her. She turned to tell Benjamin, but it was too late. He was already stumbling half-asleep on his way to bed.

Every day people passed by on the road in front of the Gannett farm. One man Deborah knew on sight was Paul Revere, a stocky broad-shouldered man, and war hero famous for his midnight ride. One pleasant afternoon, the silversmith stopped at her gate. She let his horse drink from a bucket of water she drew from the well.

"I've been hearing people talk about you serving in the war. Are those stories true?" he wondered.

Deborah talked to him while she weeded the garden. It wasn't long before he dismounted and tied his horse's reins to the gate, and began pulling weeds too. They talked about the war and the poor state of the country. Deborah told Paul she was planning to write a letter to Congress asking for her military back pay. He encouraged her. "I think you should write that letter."

But the silversmith wasn't the only one who came by the Gannett's farm. To the former soldier it seemed, almost daily, more people came up the walk to see her. They were curious and wanted to talk to Deborah about the war.

There were so many drop-in guests, it became a strain. She had to stop her chores, settle them by the fire, or at her table, and give them a cup of tea—if she had it—or brew some bitter coffee.

The year was 1797, and Deborah was thirty-seven years old. She had a household to manage, more farm work than she could physically handle, three children and two orphans to raise. All these things the former soldier did while contending with the chronic pain in her leg. The wife and mother no longer had time to sit with visitors for idle chit-chat. Knocks at the door often went unanswered.

As hard as Deborah and Benjamin worked, the farm wouldn't produce. The soil was thin and rocky. Nothing they did made a profit. Deborah noticed many of the New England farmers were having trouble, too. Most of them left their worn-out farms and moved west with their families. Deborah felt her worst fears about marriage were now realized. She felt a loss of her own independence and life force. And at times as helpless as a kitchen and stable drudge—with no stature or promise for a better life. It was a long way down from her former position as an aide to a general.

Barely able to survive financially, Deborah began writing letters petitioning Congress for back pay. She never received an answer to any of her pleas for money owed her. Meanwhile, Benjamin picked up extra work dragging timber with a team of oxen from Rattle Snake Hill to Revere's forge. But Deborah realized they were becoming poorer and poorer. Hard times were at their door, and so too was it for the new Republic. Deborah talked to one farmer who said, "I sold a cow in the spring for forty dollars. In the fall I paid forty for a goose for Thanksgiving dinner."

Money problems topped Deborah's other problem. The pain from her war wound continued to make farm and housework ever more difficult. She wondered if part of the bullet was still in her leg. She didn't know, and neither did her doctor who gave her medicine. "Oh, how I wish we had money to give the man all we owe him," she lamented. But the couple had nothing with which to pay him, except a few scrawny chickens and a jar or two of blackberry jam.

One of the curious people who dropped by to hear Deborah's stories, told her they'd read about a woman who'd also had a secret army career. The story came out on January 10, 1789, in the *New*

*York Independent Gazette*. The woman's name wasn't given, they said, but people in the colonies began to suspect the woman was Deborah. She procured a copy and read:

"A case of virtue in a female soldier occurred lately in the American Army... a lively, comely young nymph, 19 years of age... served undiscovered... in several skirmishes with the enemy, received two wounds; a small shot remaining in her to this day... she was never found in liquor, and always kept company with upright soldiers. This gallantress served as waiter to a General officer and his family. She lives eastward of Boston. She imitated a man because her parents... urged her to marry a man she had great dislike for, together with her... warm attachment to her country, she gained a reputation as a heroine... for particular reasons her real name is withheld, but the story is true."

As it turned out, Deborah heard more speculations the article had stirred up. People wanted to know the name of the mystery girl. Another newspaper named her in the headline:

"Only Girl to Fight the British, Priv. Deborah Sampson, Holden, Loves Man Who Proves Traitor."

She laughed out loud reading the untrue story of how she'd given her heart to a "wild and reckless soldier." She supposedly joined his unit to be near him. "Hogwash," she muttered, slamming the tin dinner plates down on the table.

The article had other errors: It said she taught school in Holden when she was sixteen. It gave her religion as Quaker, and said she enlisted at eighteen.

In truth, she knew her indenture lasted until she was eighteen. Although born into a Puritan family, she'd chosen to leave the Congregational Church and became a Baptist. She never taught in Holden.

Those newspaper stories fanned the flames of curiosity about Deborah and she felt their heat. But after a while, she gave up worrying about them. She knew they were about her, but her life was taken up with their struggle against poverty. *I'm settled down now, and I don't want to dig up old troubles. Some folks will get angry and make my life more miserable.*

Deborah realized from experience the people in small towns wouldn't be on her side. Of that she was certain.

# Chapter XI

## A Stranger at the Door

On a cold day in 1797, as Deborah stood lost in thought at the window, another stranger came up their walk. "I'm Herman Mann, I write for the *Village Register* in Dedham, Massachusetts. Will you talk to me about your war experiences?"

"I don't wish to talk about the war. I've left it in the past," she informed him. "Why would I want to stir up any more problems? I have trouble aplenty. Good day, Sir."

Mr. Mann left with a disappointed look on his face at her dismissal. But it wasn't long before he came back. Each time her answer was the same. Still he persisted.

After several months, Deborah grew tired of turning him away and relented. "Here, have a seat by the fire. I'll pour some tea."

Many cups of tea and visits later he asked, "May I make my notes into a book?"

"No," she sighed looking up from her weaving. "That's a bad idea. The readers would only continue to judge me. I've heard quite enough gossip to last a lifetime."

But Mann insisted. "I'll write your story as a novel—a book of fiction. No one will know it's based on your life. I'll even share the money from the book sales with you."

## Mr. Mann's Story

With Deborah's consent, Mr. Mann wrote a story about an unnamed girl in the Revolutionary War. He called it, *The Female Review: Memoirs of an American Young Lady*. When the publication came out later that year, many of its readers argued whether it was about Deborah Sampson, or not.

The former soldier found she did not like one aspect of the book—the overly embellished facts about her life. She especially disliked the ridiculous part about how the heroine fought the Indians. Deborah chastised Mann for what she felt was a fantastical narrative.

Still, she felt good because the book showed her life in a positive way. And Mr. Mann had commissioned a Mr. Stone to paint a portrait of her. "Your picture will be the book's frontispiece," he'd insisted. But in her heart the reason Deborah permitted the work to go forward was because the book sales would help to sustain her family.

During the sittings, the children sat wiggling but quiet, hands over their mouths to stifle giggles, as they looked back and forth from the painting to their mother.

When the portrait was finished, the neighbors came in to look. "Why, Mrs. Gannett, you look every bit the feminine patriot. Your long brown hair is a crowning glory, and the beaded choker adds just the right touch." When they returned home, she'd heard they also spoke approvingly of the fashionable tight drawstring sash accenting her small bosom. Still, they'd wondered if Deborah should have effected a sweeter, more demure expression. "It seems to me," one woman said, "she looks too determined."

Deborah declared, "What I like best about my portrait lies between the painting and the frame. I'm especially fond of the drawings of musket, sword and battle flag." She pointed out to the children how the emblems were further enhanced by an eagle and the Stars and Stripes. The children were so impressed with the finished painting, their mouths made little o's when they saw it.

Although Mann did not sell as many books as they'd both wished, its story fired people's imaginations. In the colonies there was much talk about it. Most praised it, but others dismissed the book as lacking substance.

But for all the hoopla, Deborah felt deeply disillusioned. The sales weren't nearly enough to bring her family out of poverty, as she'd hoped. Meanwhile her energy drained away as the pain continued unabated.

Their life became ever grimmer now as Benjamin lay sick in bed, with what she did not know. Deborah and their son Earl did their own chores, and Benjamin's as well.

*There's no way out of this desperate situation.* She wiped her eyes. She stood at the window and looked out, as she often did when troubled. Then Deborah noticed people, total strangers, gathered on her walk. It was as if they hoped to catch a glimpse of her. That's when the idea hit her. *I'll tell my story to a group of people.*

Excited, her thoughts tumbled over one another. *I'll give a speech—but where?* She scratched her head. *That's it. I'll hire a hall and each person can buy a ticket! A lecture tour—I'll go on tour!* Excited, she relayed her plan to Benjamin.

He groaned and rolled over in bed his face to the wall. Her husband muttered, "No man in American will buy a ticket to hear a woman talk. Why do you think they'd pay to listen to you? Be sensible. Stay home and take care of things here."

But Deborah knew they were starving, and it was only a matter of time before they'd be completely destitute. She imagined they'd soon be as bad off, as when her mother, and she and the other children, had been "put out on the town," charity cases. And she'd become an indentured servant. Deborah, wife and mother, was not about to let the same unfortunate thing happen to her family.

As it turned out, when she told Mr. Mann her idea, he clapped his hands. "That's a fine idea, my dear. I'll write your speech, and order you a new uniform. I'll see to it that money from additional book sales will go toward your tour expenses."

After Deborah read the speech he'd written, she objected to its style. "This is too fancy and wordy." Mr. Mann thought the speech was perfect.

"Just read it the way it's written, dear," he coaxed.

Deborah didn't like the idea of not being able to choose her own words. *He's putting words in my mouth. Why, he has me saying I'm sorry—sorry for acting unladylike.* Pshaw!

With that outburst, the older Patience looked up from her darning with wide eyes.

Deborah couldn't help herself and laughed out loud. "Isn't it ironic, Patience? I'm to apologize for acting unwomanly—while doing what no American woman has done before—receive money to speak in public."

Her adopted daughter insisted, "You go on, Mother. I'll look after the children and Mr. Gannett. Earl is nearly grown and can help with the chores. You'll make us all proud."

Deborah put her arms around Patience. "You are a treasure to us. In fact, you *are* family."

She didn't say any more to Mr. Mann about his speech. She knew what she'd do. *I'll memorize it and make the changes myself as I go along.*

But Deborah hesitated. She did not want to go against Benjamin's wishes, so she waited patiently for him to change his mind, and hoped for a miracle.

## From a Girl's Choice to a Woman's Voice
(1802 – 1803)

Women in New England began meeting together. They wanted to see if they could improve their lives. They agreed, "It's wrong for a woman's rights to end with marriage."

This change in women's attitudes inspired Deborah. Over the objections of Benjamin, she began in to plan in earnest, for her first lecture tour. She had no idea whether or not she would be successful, but she had waited long enough—but had she waited too long?

## Deborah Goes it Alone

Deborah took care of all the tour details herself. She hired the hall, and the ticket taker. She saw to the printing of notices and tickets, swept the hall, brushed the seats, and cleaned the candlesticks. She had no one to guide or help her, and no one else offered to lend a hand. As Deborah made preparations, she dreamed of how she'd soon earn money for her family by touring from town to town.

For her first series of presentations, Deborah stayed in a room at the house of Mr. Robert Williams in Boston. *The Columbian Sentinel* carried an ad about her speech. It gave the dates as March 20, 24, and 27, 1802. Finally the day arrived.

As she dressed in her uniform that evening, she thought of the first time she'd put it on. "I still look quite striking, even if I do say so," she said to her image in the mirror. She felt gratitude for her army experience. And valued the courage and confidence it gave her as she would shortly walk into the unknown.

She made her way from her room and stood outside on the walk almost unbelieving as she breathed in the sweetness of the April air. *Here I am, former indentured servant, about to give a public speech. A first for me, a first for America.*

A coach waited in front of the Williams' house, the one to take her to the Federal Street Theater. As the clip-clop of the horses' hooves drew the carriage along, she took several deep breaths and began rehearsing her speech in her mind.

Arriving at the theatre, Deborah felt an uncanny feeling of happiness envelop her. The proud soldier entered the building and saw the hall filled to capacity. A chill of pleasure ran down her spine.

Standing tall in her uniform, Deborah stepped onto the dark edge of the stage. A master of ceremonies announced her presence to the audience. A company of military officers she had chosen lined up behind her—her old friends from West Point.

Then, with all the military bearing of a Light Infantryman, she stepped into the pool of light from the great glass chandelier. A halo of warm candle light fell about her. Amid the gasps, a pleasant murmur went up from the crowd.

When the audience fell silent, Deborah spoke in a clear ringing voice without notes, without faltering, yet leaving out the apology Mann had insisted upon. Her audience listened respectfully. Yet many faces wore a puzzled expression, as if they couldn't believe what they'd just witnessed. Stunned silence enveloped the hall.

Immediately following her speech, an officer called out in a loud voice, "Mrs. Gannett, will now show her skill with a musket. She will present the manual of arms, demonstrating how the soldier's gun is moved from position to position."

As one of the officers shouted commands, Deborah began the twenty-seven maneuvers.

The drill ended with, "*Poise—Firecock!—Cock—Firelock! Take aim—Fire!—Fix Bayonet! Charge!*" People jumped to their feet and wild applause filled the hall. A man in the front row enthused, "She made the gun talk each time it came to the floor from her hand."

His comrade disagreed. "No girl can work a musket like that. Why, she's a phony... she's a boy!" He stood up and shook his fist at Deborah. The first man grabbed him and pulled him down into his seat.

To end the evening, the crowd sang, *"God Save the Sixteen States.* Deborah had never known such a marvelous evening, one filled with glowing praise—except for a few disbelievers. She tried to take it in, to soak it up.

At no time during her tour did Deborah reveal how poor she was. Nor did she mention the constant pain in her leg. Deborah did, however, become the talk of Boston.

While on her speaking tour, Deborah always wrote down all of her expenses:

"Albany, August 31, 1802

| | |
|---|---|
| To old key keeper..................................... | 2.00 |
| To Mr. Barber for printing.......................... | 3.00 |
| To Mr. Lester for finding candles................ | 1.34 |
| To sweeping the court house...................... | 0.48 |
| For cleaning the candle sticks.................... | 0.20 |
| For brushing the seats.............................. | 0.17 |
| For the dressing of my hair........................ | 1.00 |
| To boarding............................................... | 6.00 |
| To washing................................................ | 1.34 |

And she also kept track of what she earned. Deborah sent money home to the family after each speech. "Put this to good use," she instructed Benjamin.

After three Boston lectures, Deborah went home with $110—a fortune compared to how little she'd made on the farm.

Soon people in other towns invited her to speak. In May 1802 she went to Providence, Rhode Island. She wrote in her diary about speaking in Amidon Hall:

May 5... "When I came into the Hall I was pleased by the audience. They were full of unbelief—I mean my being a person that served in the Revolutionary Army. Some of them swore I was a lad of not more than eighteen years of age....

May 13... "came home to Sharon."

# Chapter XII

## On the Road Again

The money she earned never seemed to go far enough. The next spring, she felt she must go on yet another tour. And Benjamin, although no longer bed-ridden, was still too ill to do more than light chores. The family became sorely dependent on Deborah to provide for them. She could see no other choice but to venture out again.

The saddened mother hugged her children to her. They were older now, but she could see the pain in their moist, down-cast eyes when she mentioned leaving. Tears welled and then began spilling down their faces. The sight tugged at Deborah's heart. She sat them down and said, "Here's for each of you a small token of my love. Hold onto it until I return."

To Earl she gave a newly minted coin and pressed it into his palm. Then to Polly she gave the beaded choker that she'd worn for her portrait, and to little Patience, she gave one of her own fine lace handkerchiefs. To Susanna and the older Patience she gave combs and bright ribbons for their hair.

The children hung onto her hands, their arms around her waist, until she stepped into the coach. As it rolled away, she looked back watching their figures grow smaller in the distance, tears welling in her own eyes

This time the tour took her once again to Providence and Boston. She gave speeches as well in Worcester, Albany and New York City. And while in that city, she decided to visit General Paterson and his family. Deborah felt enormous gratitude to the fine gentleman and his family, and happily looked forward to seeing him once more.

General Paterson pumped her hand greeting her enthusiastically. The general's family gathered about her, excited to see her again. There were hugs all around.

Mrs. Paterson chided her, "We've been hearing about your speeches. But you're in uniform almost as much as before! "What happened to the dress, hat and shoes you left with?"

"Now, Mother, don't tease Deborah," the general said, "I want her to help me with my speech."

"Oh...are you running for office?" Deborah asked.

"Yes, I hope to be elected judge."

"I like judges." She smiled at him. "Especially, Judge Deborah."

"Yes," the general said nodding, "The woman in the Bible who's your inspiration."

Deborah rode with the general in his carriage as he spoke to crowds in New York. As their carriage whisked along the broad streets, he asked, "Well, what do you think my chances are for election?"

She gave him some blunt advice. "You'll win over more voters," she told him, "if you'd unbend. You're stiff and formal, and it scares folks. They're not military soldiers. Shake hands, and smile so that people perceive you as friendly—so they know you see and hear them." The general sputtered and threw his shoulders back, a bit offended, she thought. But when he put his new approach into action, he began drawing larger crowds and more cheers.

The former soldier also helped the general re-write his speech. She'd cut out the wordiness, but left enough punch to catch his listeners' interest.

One day as they were going about, the general asked Deborah a question so many others had asked following her lectures: How had she come to be able to do all these things, a woman alone, and Deborah answered,

"I learned how to be successful in the army. I learned how to think for myself and others, and I learned to go it alone when I had to. Going on tour was like going on a military mission. It called for planning, tactics, and a strong will. Most of all, it called for not stopping when the going got rough. And then there's my rule, which helps me have a pleasant attitude: I don't blame others for their mistakes. I don't hold anybody's feet to the fire. I've been criticized a lot in my own life. It doesn't feel good."

His eyes shown with admiration. Deborah knew they would be friends forever.

But at times homesickness got the best of her. When she was alone and thinking of her children, tears came unbidden to her eyes. In September, Deborah wrote in her diary: "O Dear, I do want to see my three dear children! Why do I say three? Have I forgotten my dear little Susanna Shepherd and Patience Payton?"

As the weeks sped by, Deborah's yearning to be with her children deepened. Although it always cheered her to read in the papers how each of her tours proved to be more successful than the last. Whenever there was time enough, she made arrangements to go home.

Deborah's character showed in her lectures, the newspapers reported. "She's a real diplomat," commented others. From Mr. Mann she heard that men in general expressed grudging admiration for her because, "She knows religion, government and military tactics." But all nodded their heads agreeing, such knowledge in a woman was not natural.

However, it was the Quakers who fully recognized a woman's right to speak in public.

## Another First for Deborah

In 1803, Deborah completely exhausted from touring, returned home for good. That was when she read the headlines, "All Soldiers Wounded in the War Receive Back Pay and Pensions." Well, they've certainly forgotten about me," she told Benjamin.

She sat down at her desk and took out her quill pen. She wrote yet another letter to Congress to remind them of her army service. Deborah continued to ask for back pay as a soldier. In each one she told of being wounded at Tarrytown, New York, "in the line of duty."

## Good Neighbor Paul Revere

On one of his many trips past the Gannett's farm to his foundry, Revere stopped by to show Deborah and Benjamin his new black horse. He'd heard from Deborah how she and Benjamin loved fine horses. His visits pleased her. She greatly admired the Revolutionary War hero. She'd told her children about his now famous, midnight ride, how in the dark of night, he rode the countryside warning the colonists that the British soldiers were coming.

It was mid1804 when he rode up to the gate, again. He stayed in the saddle as the horse cropped grass, and switched flies. As they talked, Paul gathered the horse's mane in his hand, and rubbed his other hand along its neck. All the while he listened carefully to Deborah.

"The money from the tours is gone. We used it all to pay debts." Here Deborah hesitated, "Paul, you are admired. I was only a sideshow. Meanwhile, my family is in desperate straits, again. Congress hasn't sent me what it owes."

She patted the beautiful black horse, and gave it a small lump of sugar from her pocket. "I rode a black horse when I was General Paterson's aide," she said, her eyes welling.

Deborah stalled for time. She didn't want to ask, again. It felt like begging. *But my children must have food and clothes.*

"I blush to think how much you've given me. You've done me so many good turns. Yet, I must ask once more for a loan of ten dollars. I'll pay it back as soon as I'm able," she promised.

"I know your word is good, Mrs. Gannett. I'll see what I can do."

Deborah felt her heavy heart lift. Revere was a kind man. She looked down at her hands, and then out at the distant fields. "Other soldiers have already gotten their pay and pensions long ago. Yet, my letters, all six of them, go unanswered. It's been thirteen years, and still no word."

"Yes, you may have the loan of ten dollars. But there is more I can do. I'll write a letter to Congress. You must have your money— and a pension."

On another visit to the Gannett's home, he showed Deborah the letter. "I wrote this to William Eustis. He's a member of the Congress. Here, you may read it." (It said in essence:)

Sir—
...Mrs. Gannett is ill, yet carries on as wife and mother. Her husband is good, but ill and not useful in business. They have a few

acres of poor farm land which they work together. But they are really poor.

Her ill health is a result of doing a soldier's duty. Her war wound did not heal properly.

When I heard she fought as a soldier. I thought of a tall rough woman with no understanding or education. I felt sure she was the meanest kind. When I talked with her, I saw a slender, educated woman who spoke well. She is a person who deserves a better life.

Do all in your power to aid her. She is as deserving as any man Congress has helped.

I am Sir, your humble servant,
Paul Revere

Revere's letter brought results, and Deborah's heart filled to brimming for his help. She was the first woman in America who fought in an U.S. Army uniform, to receive a military pension. The year was 1805—almost twenty years after she left the army.

Not everyone thought it a good idea. "Giving a pension— payment for former military service—to a woman is unheard of," many of the men folk grouched. "She shouldn't get a penny," the grumblers complained. Others fumed, "She'd been an outcast from the church at one time." And then there were those nasty letters to the editor that were painful for Deborah to read. Congress's agreement to give her the money owed her, did not win Deborah any friends.

When it was finally granted, Revere told Deborah he'd pick up the money in Boston for her.

"When you return," she told him, "we will celebrate."

Upon arriving in Boston he gathered the funds owed her, put them in his saddlebags and rode to Middleborough. The two friends arranged to meet at Cobb's Inn. Deborah bought him a drink to thank him.

"She drank a pint with Revere? This is an insult to women," town's folk stormed.

*Well, I've upset the apple cart again. What if Congress withdraws my pension?*

But despite the uproar, Congress let her keep the money. In 1818 the state sent $96.00 to her and said the payments would continue yearly until her death.

Victorian America, however, did not believe her story. "No woman did those things—nor would they want to," they chorused.

Feeling the sting of gossip, Deborah had a rule: "Never talk bad about anyone," she wrote to her friend the general. "I never wanted to hurt anyone, either in name, or property."

Deborah tried to make friends, but she was mostly shunned by the town's folk. Only the officers and their families befriended her.

Meanwhile, the legislature didn't mention her war wounds. They gave her a pension mainly because, they wrote, "She stayed chaste while carrying out her duties."

As a former soldier, she realized she'd fought longer than any man to receive equal pension pay. She simply never gave up. "Every woman has a right to an income when either old or disabled, and can no longer support herself," Deborah told anyone who'd listen.

## Deborah, the Grandmother

Over the years she and Benjamin continued to be amazed how quickly their grandchildren grew. The years had flown and now their children were married and had children of their own.

"Look at all these fine grandchildren, Benjamin. How many are there now?"

He laughed, "I think about twelve. But they won't hold still long enough for me to count them."

Deborah loved to have children running about the place. And they loved the stories she read to them. But their parents expressed their misgivings.

"You shouldn't be reading those awful stories to them," they admonished their mother.

"Children need stories to inspire them," she countered. "Why, where would I be if I hadn't read about Joan of Arc, and Deborah from the Bible? And you know how I loved *Gulliver's Travels*. Reverend Conant, back in Middleborough, let me borrow any book I wanted. Children need these stories so they can live strong."

It took Deborah little time to realize, in her case, fortune did not follow fame. The money remained scarce. The pension was only a pittance, and the lump-sum she was promised was never awarded.

Their house needed many repairs. They struggled with debts and doctor bills continued to pile up.

Earl, their son, unsuccessful as a farmer, become a stonecutter. He built a large new stone house in Sharon. He invited Deborah and Benjamin to live there with him and his family. Deborah's eyes welled when he offered them his home.

"Our son is a generous man," she told Benjamin.

Deborah loved the stone house. Each bedroom had a fire place and a separate parlor. When the officers and their wives visited, Deborah entertained in her own parlor. At those times she felt her old energy—and perhaps happiness—returning?

Her grandchildren appeared awed by Deborah's presence, and they liked to please her. "Thank you for bringing sticks for my fire, Benjamin," she told her smallest grandson. "Come sit by me. I've made molasses cookies today."

The little boy took a cookie from the pewter tray. Then Deborah took a cookie for herself. It made her recall baking time at the Thomases. "Soon I'll teach you to read from the *Horn Book*," she told him. "The world will open before your eyes when you learn to read—you'll see," she told him.

When Deborah entertained, her grandchildren peeked shyly through the door at the guests. "You may have a tea cake later. Remember, company first." They'd scamper away in excitement.

"Folks around here call me 'Old Soldier,'" she said as she sipped tea with her guests. My grandchildren don't understand. The war was long ago. One day, when they're older, I'll tell them about my adventures."

Patriotism was never far from Deborah's mind. Gazing out at the lawn below, she said to her grandchildren, "What this house needs now is a Liberty Tree."

"Grandmother, what's a Liberty Tree?"

"I'll show you. It's a willow tree slip—a cutting—brought over from Plymouth. That's the town our ancestors founded," she told them.

With her grandchildren, Deborah carried the willow slip out to the front yard. As they all dug together, she told them, "The willow is called 'The Liberty Tree' because it's a symbol for the Revolution."

"You told us what a Liberty Tree is," they clamored, "but what's a revolution?"

Deborah fixed them with serious eyes. "When our people stood together, united as one against repression by the Redcoats and their King. When they fought for freedom and the common good of every man, woman and child. For the good of all Americans—and our 'right to life, liberty and the pursuit of happiness.'"*

The children stood in rapt silence holding their small shovels. Then little Benjamin asked, "Grandmother, why do they call you Old Soldier? Did you fight in the war too?"

"Yes, Benjamin. I fought in the war for you and for America's independence, and found my own independence along the way. Now bring me the bucket. We need to water the willow so it will grow."

*The Declaration of Independence

# AFTERWORD

The Liberty Tree lived for nearly a hundred years. It grew to be twelve feet around. In mid-1890 a storm blew it down. The Daughters of the American Revolution carved a gavel from its wood.

Deborah died at her son's home in Sharon, Massachusetts on April 29, 1827. She was found by her son, sitting by the window a place she'd often gone when troubled. But this time there was a look of peace on her face. The former soldier had lived sixty-six years, four months and ten days. On her grave stone it simply said, "Deborah Gannett wife of Benjamin Gannett."

Her grandson Benjamin engraved a likeness of the willow tree on her tombstone.

Before she died she instructed Herman Mann, "In a second book, write the story the way it really happened." She asked him to remember the way they'd talked about it over tea. And she told Mann, she wanted Benjamin to have all the money from her book, because, she hoped, sales from Mann's second book would help her family when she was gone.

She thought about the pension money, too. Deborah insisted if she were to go first, Benjamin must file for a pension. He was, after all, a widower of a soldier.

Benjamin is said to have responded with a chuckle, "Oh, my dear, don't be silly. That's never been done before."

Then Deborah spoke her truth. "That's never stopped me, Benjamin, and it shouldn't stop you." They'd both laughed at the reality of it.

In time, her husband asked his neighbors, "I'm a widower. Do you think I should get a pension same as a widow?" They all agreed, and he wrote a letter to the state.

The lawmakers took a long time to talk it over. In 1838, they sent him $466.60. But Benjamin died before it reached him. (It was thought the money eventually was divided among the children.)

John Quincy Adams had heard about Deborah's struggle for a military pension. Also, his wife Abigail sent letters reminding him "to remember the distaff side." Ten years after Deborah's death, he said, "I am against slavery. But I am for the rights of women. We must listen to women's voices, or I fear for their wellbeing."

People were surprised. The President had taken up the woman soldier's cause. And it may well be Deborah was the forerunner of those women who in 1848, at Seneca Falls, held a women's rights convention.

## America Honors Deborah

Julia Stickney, a national historian, preserved Deborah's history. She notes Deborah has been honored in these ways:

• In 1797 Phillip Freneau, known poet of the Revolution, scolded rich politicians for ignoring Deborah's pension request and wrote an "Ode" to Mrs. Gannett, "A Soldier Should Be Made of Sterner Stuff."

• In 1944 one of the liberty ships (cargo ships) designed for emergency construction in WWII, was named the "Deborah Gannett," and launched at Baltimore.

•The first Freedom Train, 1948-49, carried Deborah's 1818 request for a military pension papers, and was seen by millions of Americans across the nation. (The engine for the train was from Fort Worth, Texas.)

•In 1976 the song, "Deborah Sampson" was sung in her honor by the Fort Worth, Texas Boys' Choir, for the American Bicentennial.

•There is a bronze statue of Deborah in front of the Sharon Library.

•Her name is on a plaque at the U.S. National Cemetery.

• In 1997, *Song of Deborah*, was sung for women veterans at a memorial service.

• In March of 1999, President Clinton said in a speech, "Deborah Sampson was one of the women who shaped our destiny and enriched our society."

• 2011 The National Women's History Museum's online education and resource website includes Deborah Sampson in a list of American heroes at http://www.nwhm.org.

## By Her Own Lights

Deborah was unique for her time. Yet, she added an important dimension to the new Republic—the equal worth of women. She knew as well as anyone great feats call for great risks—whether it be man or woman.

Pioneer women, who came after Deborah, crossed the country to live in the West. They had the same curiosity, will and spirit. They lived by their own lights. Like Deborah they showed the same kind of grit, the same brand of courage.

Many years later a grandson, George Washington Gay, had a memorial stone marker made for her. While she lived, he never knew she became the first American woman to go on a paid public lecture tour. And it would be as Historian Catherine Brekus said, "Only the Quakers fully recognized a woman's right to speak in public."

The memorial at Rock Ridge Cemetery, Sharon, Massachusetts reads;

Deborah Sampson Gannett
Robert Shurtliff The Female Soldier
Service 1781-1783

In April, 1902, a dinner in the Sharon Town Hall marked the one hundredth anniversary of Deborah's first speech in Boston.

The speaker referred to Deborah as, "Sharon's prodigal daughter." He ended by saying, "It is not a question of who has the right to fight, but whether or not war is right."

Some swore they heard the echo of a merry laughter.

## Author's Last Word

In the 1990s while casually searching for my Gilbert ancestors, I simultaneously began the research and writing the story of the life of Deborah Sampson. Some years later, while working on the third draft of her story, I discovered Deborah and Benjamin's daughter, Mary, "Polly" Gannett married a Judson Gilbert on 17 March 1808. I intend at some point, to follow that Gilbert thread to see if there are stories to tell about the Gilbert descendents of Deborah Sampson. Then, too, there were the letters of a Lieutenant Benjamin Gilbert, who when he looked over Deborah's light infantry company, thought they were "all chosen men, men of sprightly genius, noble disposition and undoubted courage."

### "Ode" to Mrs. Gannett
"A Soldier Should be Made of Sterner Stuff"

By Philip Freneau
Ye Congressmen and men of weight
Who fill the public chairs
Reward this gallant Amazon,
Who for no splendid pension sues,
She asks for no proud triumphal car . . .
But something in the way of days
To cheer her heart and keep her warm;

How many bars has nature plac'd,
And custom many more
That woman never should be grac'd
with honours won from war.
All these she nobly overcame,
And taught by reason sage,

Check'd not her military flame,
But scorn'd a censuring age,
And men that with contracted mind,
All arrogant, condemn
And make disgrace in woman kind,
What honour is to them.

# GLOSSARY

**Aide/Aide-de-camp/Orderly**: a military officer acting as a confidential assistant to a superior officer

**Bayonet**: Knife to fit on the end of a rifle.

**Apprentices**: any beginner or learner who works for another

**Blue Book**: army guide book detailing rules, procedures and regulations

**Bounty**: a reward or payment for signing up to serve in the military

**Bounty Man**: a man who makes payment to those men who are recruited as soldiers

**Broadside**: a large piece of paper printed on one side, the forerunner of the newspaper

**Bundle**: anything wrapped or tied up for carrying

**Camaraderie**: a good relationship between two or more people

**Cartridges**: lead balls used in a gun as ammunition

**Continental Soldier**: a standing army of trained soldiers ready to defend the country

**D.A.R.**: The Daughters of the American Revolution (an ancestral society of patriotic people whose ancestors fought in the Revolution)

**Deacon**: a church assistant

**Draughts**: also called draft—the game of checkers

**Dowry**: money or property brought by a bride to her husband at marriage

**Epaulet**: a uniform's shoulder ornament made of straps and fringed edges

**Felon Finger**: a red callused forefinger common to women who spun or wove thread into cloth, caused by the friction of the twisting yarn

**Femininity**: female characteristic, womanhood

**Fictionalized**: part truth, part made-up story

**Flint and powder**: the striking of flint caused a spark that set off the gun powder

**Flintlock Musket**: a gunlock in which a flint embedded in the hammer produces a spark that ignites the charge or powder in the cartridge

**Garrisoned**: troops stationed at a military post or encampment

**Green**: a grassy area in the center of town

**Gruel**: a thin watery porridge or cereal

**Hardscrabble**: barren or worn-out farmland

**Haversack:** also called a rucksack. A soldier's canvas bag for carrying food, clothing, and equipment.

**Heirs**: those who receive or are willed an inheritance (goods or money)

**Impoverished**: the poor, or people who have almost nothing to live on, reduced to poverty

**Indentured**: a contract or agreement binding one person as the servant of another

**Irony**: a strange or odd coincidence

**Itinerate**: a person who moves from place to place to find or do work

**Manual Exercise**: a military arms exercise demonstrates how the soldier's weapon is moved from position to position

**Measuring Post**: each potential recruit had to stand at this post and his height measure at least 5' 5" as the rod of the muzzle-loading gun was 5 feet long

**Mentor**: a wise and trusted counselor or teacher

**Musket**: a smoothbore shoulder gun used from late 16th century through the 18th century

**Muster**: to gather men together to induct them into the army

**Muster Man**: one who assembles men to sign up them up to serve in the army

**Pension**: payment for prior military service.

**Picket Duty**: a soldier on watch or guard duty

**Queasy**: sick stomach, vomit

**Reconnaissance Missions**: scouting out the enemy

**Ruck Sack**: a canvas sack for carrying supplies

**Ruse**: an action meant to confuse or mislead the enemy

**Selectmen:** members of the city council

**Shanghaied**: kidnapped

**Skirmish**: brief fight

**Skittles**: the game of nine-pins in which a wooden disk or ball is thrown to knock down the pins

**Spinster**: a woman who has remained single past the usual age for marrying

**Tavern**: an inn for travelers to take a meal and stay the night

**Tic**: a small bundle of straw or hay

**Tinderbox**: a box to hold tinder or combustible material whose lid is used as a candle holder

**Thrash**: to beat or whip

**Tory**: a person loyal to the Crown, which was the King of England

**Variegated Cockade**: a knot of ribbon worn on the hat as a badge, giving one a "cocky" look

**Willow Slip**: a cutting from a willow tree intended to be planted

**Whig**: colonists loyal to America

# Bibliography and Acknowledgement of Sources

The following writings include both works mentioned in the text and a selection of additional materials researched in the preparation of this manuscript.

Aikman, Lonnelle, Patriots in Petticoats, "National Geographic," Vol. 148, No.4 Washington, D.C., October 1975.

"An Address 1802 by Mrs. Deborah Sampson Gannett," reprinted by Sharon Historical Society (Mass.) Introduction by Eugene Tappan, Press of H.M. Height, Boston, 1905.

Baron von Steuben, *Regulations for the Order and Discipline of the Troops of the United States*, the *"Blue Book,"* Boston, 1794.

Cheney, Cora, *The Incredible Deborah*. Charles Scribner's Sons, New York, 1967.

Dugaw, Dianne. *Women Warriors and Popular Balladry*, 1650-1850. New York: Cambridge University Press. 1989.

Eggleston, Edward. *A History of the United States and its People*, Appleton and Company, NY, 1888.

Encyclopaedia Britannica Online: Deborah Sampson, b. Dec. 17, 1760, Plympton, Mass. d. April 29, 1827, Sharon, Mass., U. S. American Revolutionary soldier and one of the earliest female lecturers in the country.

Ford, Paul Leicester, *The New England Primer*. New York, 1897.

Haskell, Mabel Percy, The Girl Who Fought In the Revolution, "Ladies Home Journal," 1960.

Herretta, James, Biographies from Early America, Unruly Women: Jemima Wilkinson and Deborah Sampson Gannett, "The Early America Review," Fall, 1996-97.

Lossing, Benson J. *Field Book of the American Revolution*. New York, 1851-1852.

Mann, Herman. *The Female Review, of Memoirs of Miss Deborah Sampson*. Ms. Mann Family Files. Dedham Historical Society, Dedham, Mass., 1830.

Massachusetts Soldiers and Sailors in the War of the Revolution. A compilation for the Archives, published by the Secretary of the Commonwealth, Boston, 1896.

McGovern, Ann, *The Secret Soldier*, Scholastic, Inc., NY, 1975.

Moody, Pauline, *Massachusetts' Deborah Sampson*, Privately published, 1975.

National Women's History Museum, Education and Resources website: http://www.nwhm.org/education resources/biography/biographies/deborah-sampson/

Norton, Mary Beth, *Liberties Daughters*, (The Revolutionary Experience of American Women, 1750-1800), Cornell Paperbacks, Cornell University Press, Sage House, Ithaca, NY, 1996.

Pierce, Grace M., Three American Women Pensioned for Military Service. "The DA Magazine," 1917. Vol.51, pages 140-222.

School Library Journal, "Deborah Sampson" song sung for the Bi-centennial by the Texas Boys Choir. Fort Worth, http://boychoirs.org/texas/tbc006.html).

Simister, Florence Parker. *A Girl with a Musket*, Hastings House, NY, 1959.

Stephens, Amanda, *Freedom at Any Price*, Grosset and Dunlop, NY, 2003.

Wachs, Eleanor, Ph.D., (Compiler and Editor,) *Deborah Sampson Gannett (1760--1827), First Woman Soldier*. The Commonwealth Museum, Secretary of the Commonwealth, William Frances Galvin, Massachusetts,1997.

Wikapedia, an online Internet source. "Women of Achievement and Herstory: Women's Military History, The Revolutionary War—1700's." http://www.undelete.org/military/timeline/.

Young, Alfred F., *Masquerade*, Alfred A. Knoff, New York, New York, 2004.

# Paul Revere's Letter

The following is a reproduction of Paul Revere's letter re:
Deborah Sampson Gannett
Canton, Feb'y 20, 1804
Courtesy of The Commonwealth Museum, Massachusetts
The Source Booklet 1997

Wm. Eustis, Esq.                                              Canton
Members of Congress                                    Feb'y 20, 1804
Washington

Sir –

Mrs. Deborah Gannet of Sharon informs me, that she has inclosed to your care application To Congress in favor of Her. My works for manufacturing copper, being at Canton, but a short distance from the Neighborhood where she lives: I have been induced to enquire her situation and Character, since she quitted the Male habit & soldier's uniform: for the more decent apparel of her own Sex, & since she has been married and become a Mother, Humanity & Justice obliges me to say, that every person with whom I have conversed about Her, and it is not a few, speak of Her as a woman of handsome talents, good Morals, a dutiful  Wife, and an affectionate parent. She is now  much out of health. She has several Children, her Husband is a  good sort of man, though of small force in business; they have a few acres of poor land which they cultivate, but they are really poor.

She has told me she had no doubt that her ill health is in consequence of her being exposed when she did a soldier's duty, and that while in the Army she was wounded.

We commonly form our Idea of a person whom we hear spoken of, whom we have never seen; according as their actions are described. When I heard her spoken of as a soldier, I formed the Idea of a tall Masculine female, who had a small share of understanding, without education & one of the meanest of her sex.-- When I saw and discoursed with (her) I was agreeably surprised to find a small, effeminate conversable Woman, whose education entitled her to a better situation in life.

I have no doubt your humanity will prompt you to do all in Your power to get her some relief. I think her case much more deserving than hundreds to whom Congress has been generous.

I am Sir, with esteem and respect, your humble servant.

Paul Revere

## About The Author

Before working twenty years as a licensed psychologist and therapist in private practice in Fort Worth, Marilyn Gilbert Komechak was on the staff of the Fort Worth Child Study Center, and was the Associate Director of the Center for Behavioral Studies at the University of North Texas. She holds degrees from Purdue, Texas Christian University and her Doctorate from the University of North Texas.

During her work as a psychologist, she also served as a consultant to schools, businesses, and corporations. She had ten articles published in various professional journals. While maintaining her private practice office, she wrote a self-help book, *Getting Yourself Together*. The CD-ROM edition was introduced at the Chicago Book Expo by Waltsan Publishing.

A second book, also published by Waltsan, *Morals and Manners for the Millennium*, was presented at the Austin Book Fair. She is a prize-winning poet and short story writer. Her poetry and short stories have been published in the U. S., Canada and Europe. Her children's book, *Paisano Pete: Snake-killer Bird,* published by Eakin Press of Austin, garnered the Oklahoma Writers' Federation, Inc. [OWFI] "Best Juvenile Book of 2003". Marilyn has participated in numerous readings and book signings in Texas. The book, *Deborah Sampson: The Girl Who Went to War*, has been well received by a readers' review panel that passed the book with high marks.

She is a member of Fort Worth Writers, the Fort Worth Poetry Society, the Poetry Society of Texas, the Fort Worth Texas Songwriters' Association, Tuesday Study Group Trinity Episcopal Church, *Who's Who of American Women*, and *Who's Who in America.*

14701609R00077

Made in the USA
San Bernardino, CA
03 September 2014